Pay at Risk

Compensation and Employment Risk in the United States and Canada

John A. Turner
Editor

2001

W.E. Upjohn Institute for Employment Research
Kalamazoo, Michigan

Library of Congress Cataloging-in-Publication Data

Pay at risk : compensation and employment risk in the United States and Canada / John A. Turner, editor.
    p. cm.
  Includes bibliographical references and index.
  ISBN 0-88099-222-0 (cloth : alk. paper) — ISBN 0-88099-221-2 (paper : alk. paper)
    1. Wage payment systems—United States. 2. Wage payment systems—Canada. 3. Compensation management—United States. 4. Compensation management—Canada. 5. Labor economics—United States. 6. Labor economics—Canada. 7. Employee fringe benefits—Finance. 8. Social security—Finance. 9. Old age pensions—Finance. 10. Insurance, Health—Finance. 11. Job security. I. Turner, John A.

HD4927.U6 P39 2001
331'.0971—dc21

2001023606

Cover design by J.R. Underhill.
Index prepared by Diane Worden.
Printed in the United States of America.

Contents

List of Figures

List of Tables

1
Introduction

John A. Turner

Major changes have occurred in the U.S. labor market over the past few decades. The rate of growth of real earnings decreased and even turned negative for periods, and earnings inequality has increased. Many observers also believe that earnings and job instability have increased.

While the decline in real earnings growth and increase in inequality are well documented, less is known about changes in earnings and job instability. Do workers bear more employment-related financial risks than in previous decades? Have work hours and pay become increasingly sensitive to the labor market? Have labor market risks in North America been shifted from employers to workers? Has there been a decline in the U.S. version of the welfare state (where employers play a relatively large role in providing social welfare benefits), just as the welfare state has declined in Europe?

CANADA–UNITED STATES COMPARISONS

Comparing Canadian and U.S. labor markets yields insights about the risks workers bear. Labor markets in the two countries have many similarities, although the relatively small Canadian economy is less than 10 percent as large as that of the United States. The proximity and dominant size of the United States cause substantial economic, cultural, and intellectual influences on Canada, and U.S. firms own a significant proportion of Canadian industry. Even before the Canada–United States Free Trade Agreement, the precursor to the North American Free Trade Agreement (NAFTA), the United States and Canada exchanged more goods and services than any other two countries in the world. Each country is the largest trading partner of the other.

Given the similarity of the two countries and their interconnections, one would expect Canadian employers to act much like their American counterparts, especially since firms from both countries often compete in the same markets using similar technologies (Verma and Thompson 1988). The similarities in the two countries and their integration through trade make it likely that the policy experiences of one have relevance for the other (Gunderson, Hyatt, and Pesando 1996).

This chapter provides an introduction to some of the conceptual issues concerning compensation risk bearing by workers in labor markets. The following discussion provides background and is more abstract than the other chapters, which discuss the evidence concerning changes in risk bearing in particular aspects of compensation. This chapter provides a framework for thinking about some of the issues raised in the more applied chapters, and it concludes with an overview of the remainder of the book.

COMPENSATION RISK BEARING IN LABOR MARKETS

Conceptual Issues

Risk is an element of all aspects of employee–employer relationships, including pay rates, working time, and employment security. The allocation of risk bearing determines the extent to which risks are borne by workers, by firms and their stockholders, and by government.

Labor market risks may pose serious problems for some workers. Many workers have mortgages and large financial commitments for rearing and educating children. Fixed financial commitments become problems for workers who face decreases in income due to unemployment or decreased work hours, or increases in expenses due to medical bills not covered by health insurance.

Employers face risks affecting their demand for labor due to changes in their factor markets, technology, exchange rates, international competition, domestic competition, the legal environment, tax policy, and macroeconomic conditions affecting demand for their product. Other demand-side factors that may affect workers' risk include factors affecting the institutional setting in which wages are set. These factors include employer size, collective bargaining status, and legal constraints (e.g., mandatory notice for layoffs).

Workers also face health-related risks that affect their labor supply, including illness, disability, declining ability to work at older ages, and early death with surviving dependents to provide for. These risks can be insured against through health insurance, disability insurance, early retirement benefits, and life insurance. Workers also face the opposite possibility of extended longevity, which brings the risk of outliving their resources, a risk that can be insured against through annuitization of retirement income.

Workers obtain insurance against risks from social insurance through government (such as social security), private insurance through employers and personal purchase, and insurance against labor demand shifts through employers and their stockholders, who may bear some labor demand risks for workers.

Risks due to the cost of health care are generally unrelated to work, but in the United States, these risks have most often been insured through health insurance provided by employers. In Canada, they have been insured through mandatory universal health insurance.

Long-term job commitments by employers provide a form of earnings insurance to workers. In spite of fluctuations in labor demand, these arrangements may benefit both workers and firms. Both workers and firms more willingly invest in workers' job skills when there is a long-term commitment. Long-term employment reduces recruiting, hiring, and training costs for employers.

Long-term job commitments by employers benefit workers in that they derive utility from the security of income, presumably accepting a lower wage in exchange for greater security. This wage reduction may be offset to some extent by higher worker productivity due to greater investments in job-specific human capital being made when there are long-term job commitments. However, if workers give up potential opportunities associated with job mobility when they enter a job that penalizes quitting, some workers may require a wage premium rather than pay a compensating differential. There is a trade-off between job security with a penalty for job change versus job insecurity with the upside potential of changing to a better job. Thus, workers who expect to have the possibility of large wage gains from job mobility will not value as highly the benefits of job security and will seek jobs that do not penalize mobility.

Policy Issues

Public policy may affect worker risk bearing. Public policy that reduces worker risk bearing may reduce work incentives, in turn reducing the flexibility of the economy and its ability to produce new jobs. Thus, public policy that increases the costs of laying off workers, such as by mandating notice of a certain length of time or mandating severance pay, may reduce risk for workers already employed but also reduce hiring by firms. Public social insurance programs may increase risk taking since they reduce its negative consequences. For example, to maintain utility constant, a worker would be willing to accept a lower level of job security if unemployment insurance is exogenously increased.

In addition, social insurance programs that provide income contingent on not working, such as unemployment insurance and old age retirement benefits, may reduce labor supply. Due to moral hazard, unemployment insurance shifts risk in labor markets toward unemployment and away from variability in wage rates. Thus, social insurance programs may increase flexibility in the labor market and may affect the form that flexibility takes. They may reduce labor supply, and the taxes to finance social insurance may strengthen that effect.

Conversely, some government policies may increase the flexibility of the labor market but at the expense of increasing risks to workers. When first elected in 1979, the British Conservative party had a stated aim of making the labor market more flexible (Millard 1997). It did this by passing legislation that reduced employment protection, eliminated the minimum wage, reduced regulations governing who could or could not be employed in various jobs, and reducing the power of unions. The length of time an employee must work before being able to take his employer to court for unfair dismissal was increased from six months to two years. New laws reducing the power of unions included a law that made it illegal for employers to refuse to hire someone because of not being a union member.

Theoretical Issues

One measure of risk is the variability in employee compensation around its expected value. This measure incorporates variability both in hours worked and in the compensation rate. Thus, it incorporates unemployment, reduction in overtime, working short hours, loss of paid hours due to ill health, variability in wage rate, and variability in nonwage compensation. This measure is incomplete, however, in that it does not cover some types of risk that pensions and health benefits insure against.

A standard decomposition of variability in earnings for an individual into permanent and transitory components is as follows:

$$Y(t) = u + v(t),$$

where Y is the log of annual earnings of individual i in year t; u is the logarithm of permanent earnings of the individual, which does not vary with respect to time; and v is transitory earnings that vary over time (Gottschalk and Moffitt 1994).

A different measure of the risks workers face is variations in the level of their consumption. For workers with little liquid savings, this measure of risk is affected by variation in both total compensation and in uninsured medical expenses. This book does not use this measure but focuses instead on more traditional measures of risk that are tied directly to labor market outcomes.

Demand-side risks can be divided into three categories.

1) Macroeconomic risk: the effects of macroeconomic fluctuations on demand for the firm's product.

2) Microeconomic risk: risks specific to the firm, industry, or region affecting demand for the firm's product.

3) Implicit contract risk relating to the firm's reaction function to macroeconomic and microeconomic risk, including changes in the insurance that firms provide against demand risk. Supply-side risk includes changes in the types of insurance the firm provides against risks, for example, pensions, health insurance, and disability insurance.

Risk bearing by firms

Firms have two considerations in designing efficient compensation contracts: incentives and risk allocation. Some employers may prefer to link pay tightly to performance because that may lead to higher productivity. It will also, however, give workers more-variable income. Insurance that cushions reductions in earnings will inevitably affect workers' decisions and behavior. Efficient labor contracts must balance risk bearing and incentives in labor markets.

A fundamental issue in determining worker–firm risk bearing is which party bears risk more efficiently, and this depends partly on which party can reduce risk through diversification at the lowest cost. Competitive labor markets equilibrate, with the party bearing risk being the one that can most cheaply do so. Both employers and employees may shift risks to insurance companies or the government. The degree to which a particular employer can pass risk back to workers is limited by the extent to which workers have the option to work for other employers that offer a better mix of risk bearing and compensation.

Employers bear risks, but the theory of compensating differentials suggests that workers pay for this through reduced wages. The implicit payments by workers inherent in reduced wages are equivalent to insurance premiums. Thus, firms with a higher probability of layoff must pay higher wages to compensate workers for this risk (Topel 1984a).

Risk bearing by employers also occurs through the implicit contract in which the employer agrees to bear some risks concerning workers' wages, hours, and employment under varying demand and profitability. Implicit (and explicit) contracts allocate risks between workers and firms, but the contracts themselves have risks for workers. An employer may break the contract, although at a cost to his reputation in the labor market.

Risk bearing is likely to vary among firms. Firms facing different labor market conditions and different financial status may adjust to shocks in different ways. Risk bearing by firms is positively correlated with firm size, due to economies of scale in managing risk bearing and the ability to diversify. Large, diversified firms may stockpile workers, absorbing transitory shocks by reducing capital expenses and reducing profits. A large firm can diversify risks more easily than can a worker, whose earnings capacity is the main component of his income portfolio. Large firms can bear risks less expensively than small firms because they have a large enough risk pool of workers that they can self-insure. By insuring most or all of their workers, large firms diminish adverse selection.

Employers' short-term adjustment strategies

Firms face fluctuations in demand for their products, but workers want stable income. In order to adjust to demand shocks, firms can reduce their labor costs. They can do so by encouraging early retirement or by reducing the hours of workers. The greater is voluntary worker turnover and retirement, the less is the risk of job insecurity due to layoffs.

An aging workforce may have a positive effect on job security because there would be greater flexibility due to retirements. A labor force with a high proportion of young workers would also be more flexible because there would be greater turnover due to the relatively high turnover of young workers. The demographic composition of the labor force thus may affect the extent of job risk workers face. A middle-aged worker would face less job insecurity in a firm with a high proportion of its employees being young or being near retirement. Thus, there may be an increase in job insecurity in the United States and Canada because the large baby boom cohort is middle aged, and there are relatively few younger and older workers.

Employers can reduce fluctuations in employment by increasing or reducing overtime or short time. An alternative approach is to hire temporary employees during periods of peak demand. Hiring temporary employees may help preserve the job stability of long-term employees. Abraham and Houseman (1993) suggested that having broadly trained employees who can be transferred into the positions of workers who are quitting or retiring is another form of short-term adjustment.

For several reasons, firms may prefer layoffs to reducing hours. With layoffs, they can economize on fixed costs of employment, such as providing health insurance for their employees. With layoffs and experience-rating of unemployment insurance premiums, the employer's future costs increase. Because experience-rating is less than perfect, however, unemployment insurance may provide a way of shifting costs to other employers.

Abraham and Houseman (1993), however, argued that adjustments to varying labor demand through hours worked are superior to adjustments of employment, especially when the varying demand is cyclical. Employment adjustments entail more fixed costs (e.g., subsequent hiring costs) than do hours adjustments.

The extent to which firms adjust their labor demand by hiring and firing workers is affected by the fixed costs they face for hiring and firing, including the costs of training workers. Millard (1997) modeled labor market flexibility as depending on the fixed costs employers pay when creating or destroying jobs. An increase in fixed costs of hiring and firing leads to greater average hours worked, lower employment, and thus more use of full-time workers and less of part-time workers. Advance notice and severance pay provisions for layoffs are an aspect of fixed costs.

Employers can adjust compensation by reducing wages, reducing bonuses, and reducing nonwage compensation. In Japan, a fairly large percentage of pay in large firms is received through twice-yearly bonuses. Fluctuations in bonuses allow Japanese firms to maintain a stable workforce in the face of fluctuating demand. Small fluctuations in pay in the United States can occur through profit-sharing plans, where the employer does not commit to regular contributions but only contributes depending on the profit received by the firm.

To the extent that wages and compensation are inflexible downwards, more of the adjustment in labor demand will occur through changes in hours, including short-time and layoffs. Downward flexibility in wages requires renegotiating wage contracts. For reasons that are not well understood, it appears to be difficult to renegotiate wage contracts, which inhibits wage flexibility. Thus, when negative productivity shocks occur, adjustments tend to be made through hours of work rather than through wages.

Because of downward nominal wage rigidity, it may be easier to adjust real compensation during periods of inflation when real compensation automatically declines in the absence of action taken by employers.

Risk-averse workers are not indifferent to these options and would presumably prefer small compensation cuts or temporary layoffs to job loss, but, with unemployment insurance, they would prefer layoffs to large compensation cut. The provision of more generous unemployment insurance benefits increases the likelihood that employers will respond to adverse demand shocks with layoffs (Feldstein 1976; Topel 1984b). Eberts and Stone (1992) found that employers in the United States initially adjusted employment rather than wages in response to economic disturbances.

If they can cheaply store their product, firms can continue production at a constant level and adjust to a decline in demand that is expected to be temporary by stockpiling their product. With the development of just-in-time delivery, resulting in less stockpiling of inventory, there may be greater sensitivity of labor demand to product demand. In most modern economies, however, labor demand is closely tied to product demand. When labor demand falls, a decline in pay from a job could provide a buffer that reduces the risk of layoff.

Shocks to labor demand can be borne by stockholders. The extent to which they are borne by stockholders depends in part on the willingness of stockholders to do this and in part on the level of profits. Gordon (1982) hypothesized that the larger share of nonlabor income in Japan than the United States helps explain how large Japanese firms can offer their employees employment stability.

The apparent increase in job instability in the United States, however, has occurred at the same time that profits have grown relative to GDP. This pairing of events raises the question, have stockholders found it profitable to shift risk to workers? At the same time, have other factors (such as increased competition) reduced the level and stability of profits for some firms, reducing their ability to bear risks for workers?

There is a trade-off between volatility in compensation and volatility in employment. However, to the extent that real wages fall as an adjustment to a decline in demand, some workers may voluntarily quit. Workers who are laid off or quit may adjust by migrating to a different part of the country where they view their prospects to be more favorable, although this is done mostly by young or highly skilled workers. Thus, it may be more difficult for older workers to adjust to an increase in job insecurity than for younger workers because the costs of geographic mobility tend to be greater for older workers.

THE APPROACH OF THE BOOK

The primary question this book addresses is as follows:

Are U.S. and Canadian workers bearing greater financial risk related to employment than in the past? This question provides the book's unifying theme, with the emphasis being on explaining changes in risk bearing. The approach used to address this question involves three further questions:

1) Do U.S. workers bear greater financial risks than Canadian workers?

2) Do the trends in risk bearing in the two countries differ?

3) What should be the policy responses in Canada and the United States?

To answer these questions, we examine changes in the variability in compensation, hours and employment, and changes in employee benefits and labor market programs. Each chapter discusses, as relevant, changes that have occurred in the United States and Canadian economies, theoretical issues, the economic literature relating to those changes and risk bearing, and the policy issues and implications. Taking a broad perspective, the book synthesizes research on risk bearing in various aspects of compensation, where previously changes in risk bearing have been discussed in isolation.

OUTLINE OF THE BOOK

Risks to Wages: The Traditional and Contingent Workforces

Chapter 2: Wage and job risk for workers

Aspects of job insecurity include the duration and incidence of unemployment, involuntary nonstandard work, and short-tenure jobs. Chapter 2 examines the question, has worker risk concerning hours, wages, and employment increased in traditional employment relationships in the United States and Canada? Some analysts have suggested that workers have less job security than in the past because of rapidly changing technology and, to a lesser extent, growing international trade. The result has been downsizing by firms, flattening of management structures with layoffs of middle management, and fewer manufacturing jobs. Has the implicit contract between workers and firms changed so that firms no longer promise the degree of job security they once did?

Aggregate U.S. labor market statistics, however, indicate little overall increase in job instability. Job instability (measured by median completed tenure, estimated retention rates, and job turnover) has been stable or increased for much of the labor force and decreased for other parts of the labor force.

Job insecurity, however, has increased for older males. Median tenure for males in age groups above age 40 has declined considerably. Median tenure declined in all educational categories for this age group, and other measures of job stability for this age group also declined.

While unemployment rates have decreased to historic lows for some groups, the proportion of displaced workers that are white collar has increased. Perhaps connected to the pattern of job instability by age and by being a white-collar worker; long-term unemployment (longer than 15 weeks) has risen as a percentage of total unemployment, because it is more difficult for this group to find new employment.

Job insecurity is particularly serious for midcareer workers age 40 and older. These workers have financial responsibilities for families, and because of their accumulation of firm-specific human capital, the wage loss from a layoff and subsequent hire by a different employer is greater for a worker in his or her peak earnings years than it is earlier in life.

Chapter 3: Risk in employment arrangements

Nonstandard work arrangements include contingent, alternative, and part-time workers. This chapter indicates that, relative to the size of the labor force, the growth of the contingent and alternative workforce has been slight.

Many workers, however, do not have the type of employment relationship they prefer. While some workers prefer the flexibility of nonstandard work, roughly half of contingent workers surveyed indicated that they preferred noncontingent work arrangements. Houseman (1995) noted that the rate of involuntary part-time employment, those who desire full-time work but cannot find it and those temporarily put on short-time work by their employer, has increased. While many think self-employment has increased due to downsizing and is itself a symptom of increased job insecurity, labor statistics indicate otherwise. The percentage of workers who are self-employed has been fairly stable since 1980 (Bregger 1996).

An unanswered question related to this chapter is, has the cost of providing health and pension benefits in the United States caused firms to increase the hiring of contract and temporary workers, for whom they need not provide benefits?

Risks in Nonwage Benefits

Chapter 4: Health and coverage at risk

Employee wages and salary are about 70 percent of compensation for private industry workers. Many of the risk-bearing aspects of compensation are connected with the nonwage 30 percent. Chapter 4 discusses changes in worker and retiree health insurance affecting worker risk bearing.

Health insurance plans in the United States are becoming less generous, with higher deductibles and higher copayments, they also cover a smaller percentage of the workforce. In this aspect of compensation, U.S. workers bear more risk than previously and bear greater risks than do Canadian workers. Because health insurance in the United States for individuals younger than age 65 is provided primarily through employers, loss of a job also often means loss of insurance. This connection makes job insecurity a more serious problem for older workers than for younger workers because the need for health insurance is greater for older workers. It also causes job insecurity to be a more serious problem in the United States than Canada.

In Canada, substantial health care benefits are provided through government programs. Many employers, however, provide supplementary health benefits. As the Canadian provincial governments struggle with the costs of medical care programs, employers are increasingly being asked to bear the cost of the benefits. Due to their own budgetary limitations, Canadian employers are incorporating cost containment features into their programs.

Chapter 5: Risk sharing through social security retirement income systems

Social security old-age benefits are an important aspect of employment-related risk bearing. They affect workers' risks with respect to their employment-related retirement income. The social security systems in Canada and the United States are similar in many important respects. They both are defined benefit systems with partial advance funding. They both provide benefits based on career average wage-indexed earnings. They both provide modest benefits as compared with systems found generally in western Europe. An important difference between the two social security systems is that, in addition to earnings-related benefits, Canada provides non-earnings related benefits as an important part of the retirement income system. These demogrants are not provided in the United States. Because of these demogrants, the chapter characterizes the Canadian system as a four-tier retirement income system (demogrant, earnings-related social security benefits, private pensions, and private savings) while the U.S. retirement income system is generally characterized as a three-tier system (social security, private pensions, and private savings).

This chapter indicates that the Canadian social security system is generally more progressive than is the U.S. system, both in terms of financing and in terms of benefits. It generally provides better insurance against low earnings. For most women who have worked in paid employment, social security in Canada provides better survivors benefits, relative to benefits received while the spouse was alive, than it does in the United States.

Chapter 6: Risk bearing in individual and occupational pension plans

This chapter analyzes the trend towards workers bearing more risk in pension benefits in the United States and Canada and analyzes whether there is greater risk to pension benefits in the United States or Canada.

Financial risk is inherent in pension plans. It must be borne—by workers, the employer, an insurance company, stockholders and bondholders of the company, taxpayers, or by other employers.

The rules that specify the conditions of benefit payment determine who bears pension risk. Some rules are explicit, determined by law, collective bargaining, or the pension benefit formula. Others are implicit, for example as to when the firm will provide cost-of-living adjustments to retirement benefits or terminate the pension plan.

Pension risks arise due to nondiversifiable investment risk in defined contribution plans and to variability in defined benefit liabilities caused by changing interest rates. Pension risks for workers arise due to uncertainty as to labor supply and demand, uncertainty as to life expectancy, inflation risk, and "political market" risks arising due to changing pension regulations. They also arise due to financial malfeasance in pension fund management.

Pensions also insure workers against risks. For example, an annuitized pension insures against the risks of outliving ones resources or of being unable to work in old age. As seen in this chapter, many employees are bearing more risk due to the change from defined benefit to defined contribution pension plans.

Chapter 7: Risk shifting in workers' compensation

Chapter 7 discusses changes in workers' compensation and how those changes affect risk bearing. Workers' compensation is financed by employers through premiums paid to insurance companies or through payroll taxes in jurisdictions where there is a monopoly state insurer. The ultimate incidence of at least part of these costs is passed on to workers in the form of compensating wage or benefit reductions. Thus, increased costs of workers' compensation associated with increased risk of injury or disease have always been borne to some extent by workers. An important question is, have pressures increased to shift a greater amount of risk associated with workplace injury and disease to workers?

There are reasons to believe they have. Intensified competition in product markets and freer mobility of capital resulting from increased foreign competition restrict the ability of employers to pass some costs of work injuries on to consumers in the form of higher prices. The full costs of workplace injuries may have been increasingly shifted to the factor of production whose mobility is largely circumscribed: labor.

In response to growing workers' compensation costs, legislators in both the United States and Canada have begun to limit both the availability of benefits and the magnitude of the generosity of the benefits that are awarded, with the effect of shifting costs more directly to workers. In both the United States and Canada, workers' compensation rules have restricted access to benefits for certain injuries. In Canada, a number of jurisdictions have reduced the income replacement rate for temporary and permanent partial disability benefits.

Workers' compensation arose out of a compromise in response to the uncertainty for both employers and workers of tort actions over work injuries. The no-fault system that evolved restricted the rights of workers to sue their employers for compensation of work injuries in return for adequate benefits paid with certainty. However, to the extent that regulators reduce the injuries and diseases that are covered by workers' compensation statues, possibilities open for increased litigation over workplace-related ailments.

CONCLUSIONS

This book analyzes many aspects of risk bearing by workers in Canada and the United Sates. Workers face many risks concerning their labor market earnings. Their compensation can vary due to variations in hours worked (including unemployment), real wage rates, and nonwage compensation and social insurance (such as pensions or health insurance). Within a given level of compensation, the insurance provided by employers can vary due to changes in the circumstances under which payments are received and the value of those payments. Employers can change the structure of pensions and (in the United States) health insurance or eliminate those benefits. The insurance protection provided by government may also vary, with changes in the provisions of social security programs and their levels of benefits.

Some of these factors affecting the level of financial risk workers bear fluctuate cyclically, others are subject to long-term trends, and others have both cyclical and trend elements to their variations. In the discussion in this book, an attempt is made to separate cyclical and short-run changes from trends and focus on the latter.

In addition, an attempt has been made to separate changes in worker behavior from changes in risks. For example, the labor force participation of women had become more like that of men, with an associated decrease in women's labor force turnover. This does not necessarily indicate that job risks for women have decreased. The evidence on job turnover for men suggests that job risks for older men have increased. Presumably, a similar effect for older women has been masked by their increasingly strong attachment to the labor force.

While not all trends affecting worker financial risk are moving towards greater financial risk bearing by workers, a number of trends are moving in that direction.

1) Job turnover has increased for older male workers. This is a group for whom involuntary job turnover is particularly expensive.

2) There has been a decline in insurance provided through nonwage compensation in the form of employer-provided health insurance in the United States and defined benefit pensions.

3) There has been a small increase in the percentage of workers in the contingent workforce.

4) Changes in social security have increased financial risk bearing by workers.

5) Many recent workers' compensation legislative reforms have caused workers to bear a greater direct burden of the costs of workplace injuries and illnesses.

The Canadian economy is greatly affected by changes in the U.S. economy. In Canada, however, the effects of job insecurity are less severe because of more generous unemployment benefits and because health insurance is not tied to employment.

While many hypotheses concerning causes and effects of changes in risk bearing have been discussed, and an attempt has been made to synthesize existing research on disparate subjects, this broad and complex subject eludes our full understanding. Much work remains for future researchers.

References

Abraham, Katherine G., and Susan N. Houseman. 1993. *Job Security in America: Lessons from Germany.* Washington, D.C.: The Brookings Institution.

Bregger, John E. 1996. "Measuring Self-Employment in the United States." *Monthly Labor Review* January/February: 3–9.

Eberts, Randall W., and Joe A. Stone. 1992. *Wage and Employment Adjustment in Local Labor Markets.* Kalamazoo, Michigan: W.E. Upjohn Institute for Employment Research.

Feldstein, Martin. 1976. "Temporary Layoffs in the Theory of Unemployment." *Journal of Political Economy* 84(October): 937–958.

Gordon, Robert J. 1982. "Why U.S. Wage and Employment Behavior Differs from that in Britain and Japan." *Economic Journal*   92(December): 13–44.

Gottschalk, Peter, and Robert Moffitt. 1994. "The Growth of Earnings Instability in the United States Labor Market." *Brookings Papers on Economic Activity.* 2: 217–254.

Gunderson, Morley, Douglas Hyatt, and James E. Pesando. 1996. "Public Pension Plans in the United States and Canada." Prepared for the W.E. Upjohn Institute Conference on Employee Benefits, Labor Costs, and Labor Markets in Canada and the United States, November 4–6, 1994.

Houseman, Susan N. 1995. "Job Growth and the Quality of Jobs in the U.S. Economy." Staff working paper 95-39, W.E. Upjohn Institute for Employment Research, Kalamazoo, Michigan.

Millard, Stephen P. 1997. "The Effects of Increased Labour Market Flexibility in the United Kingdom: Theory and Practice." Unpublished manuscript, Bank of England.

Topel, Robert. 1984a. "Equilibrium Earnings, Turnover, and Unemployment." *Journal of Labor Economics* 2(October): 500–522.

———. 1984b. "Experience Rating of Unemployment Insurance and the Incidence of Unemployment." *Journal of Law and Economics* 27(April): 61–90.

Verma, Anil, and Mark Thompson. 1988. "Managerial Strategies in Canada and the U.S. in the 1980s." In *Industrial Relations Research Association Series: Proceedings of the Forty-first Annual Meeting*, New York, December 28–30, pp. 257–264.

2
Wage and Job Risk for Workers

John A. Turner

"No-cut contracts are history. Permanent jobs are long gone. Job security is a thing of the past." (*Calgary Herald*, February 18, 1996)

Many Canadians and Americans believe that job insecurity has increased, with ties of loyalty between employers and employees weakening. This opinion has been expressed during the late 1990s in the Canadian and American press as well as by politicians in both countries. Public opinion polls in the United States have shown that workers believe job insecurity has increased (Schmidt 1999).

Inspired by popular concern, economists have begun investigating this question. More studies have examined labor markets in the United States than in Canada. The evidence from the studies has been mixed.

In recent years, most insights of economics concerning employment, unemployment, and wage determination have resulted from an implicit contract approach. This approach is based on the presumption that long-term relationships between workers and firms enhance productivity for many skilled jobs. Part of the implicit contract may be the promise that firms bear some risks for workers—sheltering workers from employment and wage effects of shifts in supply and demand, at least for shifts up to a certain magnitude and expected duration. Job insecurity could increase if the implicit contract has shifted risk from firms to workers.

Alternatively, with no change in implicit contracts, job insecurity could increase because of greater macroeconomic fluctuations or greater inherent instability in the labor market. Some analysts have suggested that workers have less job security than in the past because of rapidly changing technology and increased competition due to deregulation and the growing importance of international trade. The result has been downsizing by firms and flattening of management structures.

This chapter examines whether job and wage insecurity have increased in Canada and the United States. Aspects of job insecurity are discussed for Canada and the United States separately and then compared. The chapter examines empirical evidence over the past several decades to gain insights on the causes of job insecurity. It also examines more recent empirical studies to assess changes in job insecurity during the 1990s. Both cyclical and long-term causes of job insecurity are assessed. The chapter concludes that, by some standard measures, the increase in job insecurity has been slight. A closer examination, however, indicates a hidden increase. Job insecurity measured as involuntary job separations has clearly increased for some groups. Moreover, the increase in the cost of job insecurity may have been considerable because the job loss has been particularly costly for the people affected.

CANADA

Macroeconomic Instability

Greater job insecurity could result from greater instability in the macroeconomy. Evidence from past decades may shed light on the mechanisms.

Altonji and Ham (1987) examined the hypothesis that the aggregate economy in Canada was more unstable in the 1970s and early 1980s than in the 1960s, focusing on the variance of aggregate Canadian employment growth. They compared that variance over the periods of 1963–1970 and 1972–1982. They examined the effects of shocks arising from the U.S. economy, as well as other shocks to the Canadian national economy, particular industries, and provinces. They found that changes in U.S. GNP dominated, accounting for 65 percent of the variance in Canadian employment growth. The variance in national employment growth doubled in the 1970s and early 1980s as compared with the 1960s. The increases in the variances of various shocks, largely the increase in the variance of the U.S. GNP, led to the greater instability of aggregate Canadian employment growth in the 1970s and early 1980s. Thus, their findings suggest a causal link between labor market instability in the United States and Canada and an increase in labor market instability in both countries.

Job Turnover

Greater instability of aggregate employment growth could lead to greater job instability for workers. Several types of statistics can be used to indicate whether job instability has increased. These include data on job tenure, job retention rates, job turnover, and part-year work. These measures can be divided into two general types: those that measure how long individuals have worked in a particular job and those that more directly measure employer-induced job instability.

Job instability most simply could be measured as the probability that a worker would terminate a job (quit or be laid off) during a period. This measure of job instability indicates the amount of job change in the economy but does not indicate the degree of job risk or insecurity a worker faces. When conditions in the labor market are favorable, workers are more likely to change jobs voluntarily.

In the 1980s, the average annual job turnover rate in Canada was 4.1 percentage points higher than it was in the previous decade. In the period of 1973–1979, the annual turnover of jobs averaged 20.5 percent in Canada, as compared with 24.6 percent during 1980–1990. The increase during the 1980s was due to an increase in both job growth and job loss, indicating that restructuring had become more important than cyclical factors (Baldwin and Rafiquzzaman 1996).

More recent work finds that both short and long (over 11 years) duration jobs increased over the period of 1979–1991 but there was little change in average duration (Green and Riddle 1997). The movement toward longer duration jobs has occurred mainly among women and appears to be due to the greater labor force commitment of married women. Green and Riddle found little change in the likelihood of long job tenure among older males, with the exception of a slight decrease in the 55–64 age range, which is perhaps attributable to some men truncating their job tenure by taking early retirement. Green and Riddle's work, at least up to the start of the 1990s, thus did not indicate an increase in overall job instability in Canada. However, they did find evidence of greater job instability for young and less educated workers and suggested that skill-biased technological change might be one explanation.

In an important paper, Baker and Solon (1999) used longitudinal Canadian income tax data reported by employers to measure earnings instability among Canadian men over the period of 1976–1992. They found growth in earnings instability over the period. The large size of their earnings panel allowed them to estimate and test richer models of earnings dynamics than could be supported by the relatively small panel surveys used in U.S. research. The Canadian data strongly reject several restrictions commonly imposed in the U.S. literature, and they suggest that imposing these restrictions may overstate the importance of earnings instability.

Unemployment

Job risk is affected by the expected duration and cost of unemployment. The unemployed in Canada faced quite different conditions in the recession of 1990–1992 than in the recession of 1981–1982 (Corak 1993). Workers who lost their jobs in the 1990s experienced longer spells of unemployment than workers did in the 1980s.

Older unemployed individuals fared considerably worse during the Canadian recession of the early 1990s, while younger individuals fared better. Workers age 45 years and older experienced longer expected average completed unemployment spells in 1992 (26.2 weeks) than in 1983 (22.8 weeks). Thus, the changing pattern of unemployment risk may cause greater job insecurity in Canada. As discussed next, however, some changes in the pattern of Canadian unemployment may be due to changes in unemployment compensation.

The Effects of Government Programs: Unemployment Insurance

The unemployment system in Canada in the late 1990s may have increased job instability while possibly increasing economic security. The system has given rise to the expression "lotto 10/42"—after 10 weeks of work, workers qualify for 42 weeks of unemployment insurance benefits. This aspect of unemployment insurance may account for the seemingly contradictory experience that both workforce participation and unemployment increased from 1972 to 1992 (Lemieux and MacLeod 1999). Both employers and employees presumably have learned how to use the unemployment system to subsidize part-year work. The Canadian unemployment system apparently has led to a significant increase in the flows into and out of the labor force in order to benefit from the generous unemployment insurance (Andolfatto and Gomme 1996).

UNITED STATES

Macroeconomic Instability

Because job instability is closely tied to the business cycle, increasing during downturns, changes in the business cycle may have an important effect on long-term changes in job stability. Conventional measures of the U.S. business cycle indicate that the average expansions since World War II have been twice as long as they were in the pre-war period and contractions have been half as long. Watson (1994) suggested three possible explanations for these trends. First, shocks to the economy have been smaller in the post-war period, possibly as a result of either fortuitous economic change or effective government policies dampening the effect of exogenous shocks. Second, the composition of output has shifted from cyclical to less cyclical sectors. Third, the apparent stabilization is largely spurious, caused by the way that pre-war and post-war business cycle reference dates were chosen by the National Bureau of Economic Research (NBER). He presented evidence suggesting that the third explanation is the cause, largely due to the poor quality of data in the pre-war period. He concluded, however, that while business cycle downturns have remained constant in average length when calculated using a consistent methodology, their amplitude has decreased. His study, however, predates the record-breaking economic expansion of the 1990s and early 2000s.

Other analysts have found diminished cyclical macroeconomic fluctuations in the post-war period in the major economies of the Organisation for Economic Co-operation and Development (OECD), including the United States and Canada (Bordo, Jonung, and Bergman

1998). This has been interpreted as evidence that counter-cyclical policy has been more effective in the post World War II period than before. An additional explanation is that increased integration of the world economy mitigates the negative influence of any one country's disruptions on other countries. The correlations among real output in 13 advanced countries have increased over time, suggesting a more integrated world economy (Bordo, Jonung, and Bergman 1998).

Changes in macroeconomic stability affect job stability but are only part of the causes of overall job stability. Most plant- and establishment-level employment fluctuations are idiosyncratic and are not explainable by macroeconomic or sectoral shocks (Dunne, Roberts, and Samuelson 1989).

Fluctuations in Wage Rates

The United States has traditionally been considered to have downwardly inflexible wages. In comparison to Japan and Great Britain, for example, it has been considered to have less flexible wages and more flexible employment (Gordon 1982). When wage rates are flexible, shocks that might cause job loss can be absorbed through wage rate reductions. Thus, changes in wage flexibility affect employment stability, but they may also be affected by changes in the underlying volatility of demand for labor.

While low inflation is a goal of macroeconomic policy, moderate inflation may provide a degree of flexibility in real wages when nominal wage rates are downwardly inflexible. A very low rate of inflation may thus reduce the ability of firms to adjust their compensation levels in responses to fluctuations in demand. With the rapid U.S. inflation of the 1970s, firms could deal with competitive pressures by granting nominal wage increases below the rate of inflation, thereby reducing real costs without nominal wage cuts or layoffs (Levy and Murnane 1992). The low inflation of the mid and late 1990s could be a source of greater job instability because that form of real wage adjustment is greatly reduced.

Earnings Instability

One dimension of labor market instability is instability in earnings. Gottschalk and Moffitt (1994) used the Michigan Panel Study on Income Dynamics to examine instability in annual earnings. They examined a sample of white males ages 20–59 over the years 1970–1988. They determined permanent earnings by calculating an age-earnings profile for each worker and then calculating transitory earnings in each period as the difference between actual earnings and the predicted earnings of the worker's age-earning profile. They further decomposed transitory earnings into transitory fluctuations of real weekly wages and annual weeks of work. Comparing earnings between 1970–1978 and 1979–1987, they found that the transitory variances of both real weekly earnings and annual weeks of work had increased. Roughly half of the increase in the variance of transitory earnings was due to an increase in the variance of weekly earnings. The percentage of men with large transitory fluctuations rose particularly dramatically.

Nonunionized workers had substantially higher transitory variances in earnings than unionized workers, suggesting that the shift away from unionization is part of the reason for the increase. The transitory variances for both groups increased, however, in the period of 1979–1987. Similarly, the shift out of manufacturing and into service and trade jobs accounted for part of the increase, but 88 percent of the increase was due to changes within industry (including changes in unionization) rather than changes in industry composition. Before the early 1980s, the variance of transitory earnings for job stayers showed no clear trend. However, by the 1980s, fluctuations in transitory earnings were higher for both job stayers and movers. All age and education groups had increased variance in transitory earnings, but the increase was greatest among the least educated men. In sum, the increase in earnings instability is a broad phenomenon, affecting most labor force groups.

Gottschalk and Moffitt found that much of the increase in earnings instability in the 1980s was associated with large increases in job-changing rates. This finding is inconsistent with other studies that used data from the Current Population Survey (CPS) and are discussed later. They suggested that the difference between their study and other studies may be a result of differences in the wording of the questions asked in the surveys and in the samples and years covered.

Commenting on their study, Katz (1994) noted that declines in unionization and in the real minimum wage may account for an increase in earnings instability for low-educated workers.   In another study, Katz and Krueger (1991) found that deregulated industries appeared to have large increases in earnings variation.

Job Instability

In the mid and late 1990s, a large number of empirical studies focusing on the U.S. labor market addressed the question of whether job instability had increased. The studies primarily focused on the descriptive issue of whether job insecurity has increased, while not addressing the more difficult issue of why changes in job insecurity have occurred.

Studies of job tenure and job separations have been reviewed by Schmidt and Svorny (1998) and by Marcotte (1995). Some of the conflicting findings can be reconciled due to differences in the following: the way survey questions were asked, the treatment of nonresponses, the length of the lookback period over which the respondent provided information, sample selection, or the point in the business cycle when the data were collected. This survey does not attempt to reconcile the conflicting findings, but rather focuses on the areas of general agreement.

Job tenure

Aggregate labor market statistics provide little support for the widespread perception that job instability in the United States has increased. Data from the CPS show that the average length of time workers have been with their current employer has declined slightly over the past decade. Among wage and salary workers, median tenure was 3.9 years in January 1987, 4.1 years in January 1991, 3.8 years in February 1996, and 3.6 years in February 1998 (U.S. Department of Labor 1999b).

Similarly, there has been little overall change in the percentage of the workforce with long tenure (Table 2.1). A study examining data from both the CPS and from the Panel Study of Income Dynamics

(PSID), however, concluded that there was a statistically significant increase in the probability of workers having less than 10 years of tenure in both data sets over the 1980s through the mid 1990s (Jaeger and Stevens 1999).

Table 2.1 Tenure Statistics for Workers Age 20 and Over with Long Tenure, 1983–1998 (% of workforce)

Worker category	Tenure	
	10–19 years	20 or more years
All workers		
1983	18.0	8.9
1987	17.9	8.5
1991	18.9	9.4
1996	17.6	9.5
1998	17.8	9.5
Males		
1983	19.7	12.4
1987	18.7	11.6
1991	19.6	12.1
1996	17.9	11.6
1998	17.7	11.5
Females		
1983	15.9	4.9
1987	17.0	4.9
1991	18.2	6.5
1997	17.4	7.2
1998	17.9	7.4

SOURCE: Employee Benefit Research Institute compilation of U.S. Bureau of Labor Statistics data (Employee Benefit Research Institute 1999).

Tenure statistics show an increase in tenure for women and a decrease for men (Schmidt and Svorny 1998). The findings for women probably reflect the greater labor force attachment of women over time and thus may reflect a change in women's labor force behavior rather than a change in the inherent stability of their jobs. The turnover rate for women has become more like that of men as their labor force participation generally has become more like that of men.

Job insecurity has also increased for older males. Median tenure for males in age groups above age 40 has declined considerably, from 14.8 years in 1983 for men age 50–54 to 12.8 in 1991. The proportion with tenure greater than 10 years, another measure indicating long-term job relationships, has also declined for men age 40 and older. Median tenure declined in all educational groups within this age group, and other measures of job stability for this group also declined. In contrast, median tenure generally rose for age groups of women above age 40 (U.S. Department of Labor 1995b). Thus, the increase in job stability for women, possibly reflecting their labor force attachment rather than employer-side changes, may be masking an increase in job instability in aggregate labor force statistics.

Statistics on tenure for jobs in progress do not reflect eventual job tenure. Hall (1972, 1982) did the seminal work on estimating the distribution of eventual job tenure. His work was extended by Ureta (1992).

Job turnover and job retention rates

Swinnerton and Wial (1995) used CPS data to measure four-year job retention rates and showed that, on average, workers with no college education had a decline in the probability of keeping the same job for four years when comparing 1977–1983 to 1987–1991. Using the PSID, Marcotte (1994) found a similar result, as did Rose (1995) and Farber (1995).

Neumark, Polsky, and Hansen (1999) updated earlier work by calculating four-year retention rates using the 1995 CPS. They found that job stability declined modestly during the first half of the 1990s. The measured decline was reduced by the workforce shifting toward older ages in which jobs are typically more stable. While older workers tend to have more stable jobs, they found declines in job stability especially for older, more tenured workers; they also found greater declines for blacks than whites, and for men than women.

All evidence indicates an increase in job instability for black workers (Marcotte 1995). Swinnerton and Wial (1995) reported an overall decline in four-year retention rates for nonwhites from 1979–1983 to 1989–1993. Supporting results were also found by Diebold et al. (1996) and Rose (1995).

Several studies have found a decline in job stability for less-educated and low-income workers and for black male workers but an increase in job stability for women, especially more-educated women (McMurrer 1996; Swinnerton and Wial 1995; Diebold et al. 1997; Marcotte 1994; Rose 1995; Farber 1995). Job turnover rates decreased for women over the period of 1975–1995 (from 32.7 to 27.9 percent) but increased for men (from 25.7 to 26.7 percent) (Stewart 1998).

Bernhardt et al. (1999) examined job turnover for young men using data from the National Longitudinal Surveys (NLS) through 1994. They found an increase in job instability for young white men in the 1980s and early 1990s, as compared with their counterparts in the late 1960s and 1970s. Some of the increase is associated with lower marriage rates in recent years, as well as the trend towards longer school enrollment. The shift of the U.S. economy to the service sector— where jobs are generally more unstable—has also played a role. There has also been a decline in job security in manufacturing industries, probably connected with the decline in employment in those industries.

Valletta (1999) used PSID data for the years 1976–1993, combined with CPS data for the same and previous years, to measure job change. He found evidence consistent with declining employment security for all men and for skilled white-collar women. The negative effect of job tenure on the probability of dismissals has weakened over time, as has the corresponding negative effect on quits. The negative tenure effect on dismissal probabilities is reduced by employment decline in the worker's current industry.

Permanent job loss

Statistics on job tenure and job retention rates provide evidence on the stability of jobs but do not necessarily provide information on the job risks that workers bear. Job tenure and job retention are affected by both employer decisions to hire or fire and by worker decisions to stay or leave.

To study changes in job security more precisely requires isolating the effects of decisions by employers that directly affect job security. This question can be examined using measures of job loss. Events such as plant closings, an employer going out of business, or a layoff from which the worker was not recalled are considered job displacement, permanent job loss, or involuntary separation. One such measure is the percentage of the total labor force comprised of individuals whose employment ended involuntarily and who are not on temporary layoff. Excluding laid-off workers who expect to return to their previous jobs isolates those workers affected by involuntary permanent job loss. This measure includes individuals fired for cause, but they represent a small share of the total.

The concept of focusing on layoffs or involuntary job losses when discussing job insecurity has some appeal, but firms may also wish to reduce employment by encouraging workers to quit by reducing or failing to raise wages. On average, displaced workers suffer real wage losses even before they are displaced (Jacobsen, LaLonde, and Sullivan 1993).

Involuntary job loss. A total of 3.6 million workers were displaced between January 1995 and December 1997 from jobs they had held for at least 3 years. The number of displaced workers declined from 4.2 million in the previous survey of displaced workers, which covered the period from January 1993 to December 1995. Nearly half of the workers in the 1995–1997 survey cited plant or company closings as the reason for their job loss. Compared to the prior survey period, the risk of job loss had fallen for virtually every worker group, and workers displaced during 1995–1997 were more likely to be reemployed at the time of the survey and less likely to be unemployed. In the 1995–1997 survey, displaced workers who eventually found jobs spent fewer weeks without work than those who lost jobs in the previous survey. Earnings losses of workers who lost jobs during 1995–1997 were less severe than those measured in the prior survey (U.S. Department of Labor 1999a). Thus, there is considerable evidence that, consistent with unemployment being near a 30-year low, job instability in the mid 1990s had declined as compared with earlier in the 1990s (see Tables 2.2 and 2.3).

Table 2.2 Displacement Rates for Workers Age 20 and Older, 1981–1996 (% of workforce)

Year	All tenure	20+ years tenure
1981–82	5.7	2.0
1983–84	4.1	1.7
1985–86	4.0	2.1
1987–88	3.2	1.5
1989–90	4.3	1.7
1991–92	4.9	2.7
1993–94	4.4	2.4
1995–96	3.9	2.1

SOURCE: Computations from the Displaced Worker Survey by Hipple (1999).

Table 2.3 Displacement Rates for Different Demographic Groups, 1981–1996 (% of workforce)

Year	Men	Women	White	Black
1981–82	4.3	3.4	3.8	4..8
1983–84	3.2	2.9	3.9	3.9
1985–86	3.3	3.4	3.1	3.4
1987–88	2.0	2.4	2.4	2.0
1989–90	3.2	2.8	3.0	3.5
1991–92	4.1	3.5	3.8	3.8
1993–94	3.4	3.2	3.3	3.5
1995–96	2.8	3.2	3.0	3.7

SOURCE: Computations from the Displaced Worker Survey by Hipple (1999).

A number of studies have examined the longer term trends. Farber (1997, 1999) and Gardner (1995) examined whether involuntary job loss increased in the early 1990s. Both studied data from the 1980s and 1990s from the Dislocated Workers Supplements to the CPS and both found that the rate of job displacement in the early 1990s equaled or slightly exceeded that in the early 1980s, even though the latter was a period of deep recession.

Farber found that job loss rates did not decline as much as might have been expected in the 1990s given the sustained expansion. For example, the amount by which the job loss rate exceeded the unemployment rate averaged 1.2 percentage points in 1987–1989 and 3.2 percentage points in 1993–1995. The gap fell to 2.2 percentage points in 1995–1997 but remained higher than in the 1980s.

Farber found that job loss attributable to abolition of a position or shift grew from 11–12 percent of all job loss in the 1980s to 17 percent of job loss in 1991–1993. Similarly, Gardner found that the percentage of workers with at least three years of job tenure who were displaced in the early 1990s equals the percentage in the early 1980s.

Although these studies found little or no change between displacement rates in the two periods, the job displacements in the early 1980s occurred during a severe economic downturn. The displacements in the early 1990s, however, occurred during a mild recession, when displacement rates would have been expected to be considerably lower.

Farber (1997) found that most of the increase in job displacement during the early 1990s could be attributed to the increase in the percentage of workers who reported that they were displaced due to the abolition of their shift or position; in other words, what is commonly called "downsizing." The three-year job loss rate for position/shift abolished increased from 1.3 percent for 1981–1983 to 2.3 percent for 1991–1993. This increase occurred primarily for workers with at least a college education (up from 1.2 percent to 2.8 percent). In contrast, there was no general increase in displacement rates for other reasons. The rate of job loss due to plant closing has been relatively steady, and the rate of job loss due to slack work has fluctuated cyclically.

Polsky (1996) examined the trend in job loss using PSID data. He compared the 1976–1981 period with the 1986–1991 period. He found little change in job separations, but a larger fraction of separations in the later period were due to job loss. Workers aged 45–54 suffered a disproportionate increase in involuntary job loss between the two periods. Further, the reemployment probabilities for job losers decreased but not for job quitters. Job losers became more likely to suffer a large decrease in earnings, while quitters became more likely to have an increase in earnings. Thus, he found that job loss became more common in the early 1990s, and its consequences became more costly.

Borsjoly, Duncan, and Smeeding (1998) used PSID data to study the incidence of involuntary job loss among prime-age men (ages 25–59). They focused only on workers with substantial labor force attachment (held a job at least one year, worked at least 1,000 hours previous year, and not self-employed). They argued that changes in job instability are particularly important with respect to this group, which has relatively high job stability. They found that the incidence of job loss in this group increased considerably over the 1968–1992 period. It increased about as much for college-educated workers and older workers as for less educated and less experienced workers.

Gottschalk and Moffitt (1999) used the Survey of Income and Program Participation (SIPP) data to examine the year-to-year probability of job change as well as the monthly probability of job change for employed married males. These data do not show an increase in job turnover during the 1980s and 1990s. While job exit rates increased sharply in 1994, they decreased equally sharply in 1995, leaving exit rates at roughly the same level as a decade earlier. They also examined various indicators of increased insecurity, including the probability that a job ends involuntarily, is followed by a spell of nonemployment, or that the subsequent job has lower wages. None of these indicators of insecurity showed an upward trend in their data. Their results may be consistent with a decline in job security during the early 1990s followed by an increase towards the end of the decade.

Together, these studies generally indicate that the rate of employer-induced job instability was significantly higher in the early 1990s than would be expected based on the past relationship between job instability and macroeconomic conditions. In this period, job instability was higher than during the 1980s, but job loss declined in the mid 1990s.

Plant closings. Plant closings as a form of involuntary job loss may differ in their effects on workers from other causes of displacement. Hamermesh, Cordes, and Goldfarb (1987), using the PSID, presented evidence that layoffs due to plant closings are less likely to be anticipated by workers than other layoffs. For this reason, the effects of plant closings on workers may be more serious than other forms of involuntary job loss. They found that the wage-tenure profile is much steeper among workers whose plants closed than it is for those who were permanently laid off. This finding suggests that, in addition to the compensating differential for the risk of layoff, workers who actually are laid off anticipate some of their risk and respond by reducing their investment in firm-specific human capital. The same pattern of anticipation and consequent reduction in human capital investment does not appear for workers who lose their jobs as a result of plant closings.

Corporate downsizing.   As mentioned earlier, Farber (1997) found evidence of increased job displacement due to downsizing. Presumably related to this phenomenon, CPS data show that managerial and professional workers became increasingly vulnerable to job loss between the early 1980s and the early 1990s. The share of all displacements from workers in these occupations increased from 13 percent in 1981–1983 to 24 percent in 1991–1993.

In addition to an increase in the overall incidence of displacement of managers and professionals relative to total displacement, the earnings patterns of these displaced managers and professionals were also markedly different during the two periods. In the early 1980s, managers and professionals toward the bottom of the earnings distribution were disproportionately likely to be displaced. More recently, however, the earnings profile of the displaced is almost identical to that of all employed managers and professionals. This appears to be a part of the pattern of an increased cost of job instability. For managers and professionals, being at the top of the earnings ladder appears to provide less protection against job loss than it once did (U.S. Department of Labor 1995a).

Unemployment duration.   Baumol and Wolf (1996) found that the duration of unemployment remained fairly constant in the 1950s, 1960s, and 1970s and rose in the 1980s and early 1990s. When the data are disaggregated by age, the duration of unemployment increased for older workers and decreased for younger workers from the 1980s to the 1990s, indicating an increase in the cost of job instability for older workers.

Conclusions on Wage and Job Instability

The overall job tenure statistics suggest that job instability has increased slightly. Disaggregating the data by gender suggests, however, that the increase in female tenure resulting from greater labor force attachment is masking an increase in job instability, with job tenure of males declining.

A closer examination of the evidence using data on worker displacement indicates that job displacement has increased, at least for prime-age males up to the early 1990s. Involuntary job loss increased both as a share of overall job loss and relative to the size of the workforce.

Increased job displacement and decreased job tenure have occurred among groups for whom job insecurity is relatively costly. The increase in the cost of job insecurity is explored in greater depth in the next section.

The Increasing Cost of Job Loss

Perhaps a reason that worker worry over job insecurity may have increased, at least during the early and mid 1990s, is that job insecurity for more workers occurs later in life when it is more costly. It is also occurring increasingly for white-collar, managerial workers who may have considerable investments in firm-specific human capital.

In a study of displaced workers in Massachusetts, Kodrzycki (1996) found that older and more experienced workers tended to have longer unemployment periods and lower wage replacement rates when they returned to work. It is possible these extended periods of unemployment may be a result of age discrimination, and possibly because of shorter expected tenure duration at hire, older workers have more difficulty than younger workers in finding new employment.

A substantial literature uses the Displaced Worker Survey to study the postdisplacement employment and earnings experience of displaced workers. Displaced workers generally experience substantial periods of unemployment and their earnings on jobs held after displacement are substantially lower than predisplacement earnings. The earnings loss suffered by workers is positively related to tenure on the predisplacement job.

Polsky (1996) used the PSID to examine changes in the cost of job loss between 1976–1981 and 1986–1991. Controlling for personal characteristics, he found a statistically significant decline in the probability of reemployment of 6.1 percentage points between the two periods and an increase of 2.3 percentage points in wage losses with job loss between the two periods. Workers who experienced a significant increase in wage losses with job loss between the periods examined include older workers, professional and managerial workers, and high-tenure workers.

Farber (1999) found that proportional wage losses of job losers are lower in the most recent period he examined (1995–1997) for all workers except those in the lowest educational category. Thus, the cost of job loss declined for the average worker that lost a job towards the end of the 1990s.

Because of their accumulation of firm-specific human capital, the wage loss from a layoff and subsequent hire by a different employer is greater for workers in the peak earnings years than for younger workers. Hamermesh, Cordes, and Goldfarb (1987), using the PSID, estimated that involuntary separation causes a loss of firm-specific human capital equivalent to more than six months' wages. The value in terms of months' wages is higher for high-wage workers at the peak of their earnings profiles. Thus, the value of lost earnings is large, especially for employees with long tenure who are still years away from retirement. Data on worker displacement suggest that long tenured workers displaced due to the closing, reorganization, or relocation of a business or plant typically suffer larger earnings losses after displacement than do otherwise similar workers displaced with short tenure (Carrington 1993).

Because of their accumulation of human capital, their loss due to depreciation of human capital during unemployment is also greater. Human capital depreciates during unemployment as workers' skills and knowledge erode. Perhaps in part for this reason, Farber (1999) found that high tenure workers suffer dramatically larger earnings declines than do workers with less tenure.

Job insecurity is particularly serious for midcareer workers in their forties and early fifties for a number of additional reasons. These workers often have financial responsibilities for families and fixed financial commitments for mortgages and children's education. The increase in job loss at higher tenure has thus increased the cost of the risk of job loss for workers.

The forties and fifties are also particularly costly ages for workers to lose pension coverage. The pension wealth loss caused by a separation from a job providing a defined benefit plan is greatest for a worker roughly 10 years from retirement (Turner 1993). At that point, the worker has accumulated substantial pension wealth, but that wealth is generally based on the nominal value of his or her final wage. Inflation could erode the real value of the final wage over a 10-year period. Thus, a worker aged 50 losing a job with a defined benefit plan could suffer a large pension wealth loss.

A further reason for the increase in the cost of job loss is the increase in permanent job loss relative to temporary job loss. Davis, Haltiwanger, and Schuh (1996, p. 138) found that the dominant role of permanent layoffs in the recession of the early 1990s suggests that job destruction persistence rates were high during that recession. The phenomena of prolonged, persistent job destruction and the larger role of permanent layoffs since the early 1980s are linked to the rise in long-term joblessness.

U.S.–CANADIAN COMPARISONS

Job Creation and Destruction

While job tenure and job turnover statistics present job instability from the viewpoint of the worker, job creation and destruction look at the process from the viewpoint of the employer. *Job creation* refers to the number of jobs created at plants where employment is growing and *job destruction* to the number of jobs ended at plants where employment is shrinking. Davis, Haltiwanger, and Schuh (1996, p. 21) compared job creation and destruction rates in Canada and the United States. The rates they used for Canada were for the 1979–1984 period;

the rates for the United States were for the longer 1973–1988 period. The rates for both countries are for manufacturing firms. The job creation rate was higher at in Canada (10.6 percent versus 9.1 percent), and the job destruction rate was slightly lower in Canada as well (10.0 percent versus 10.2 percent). There was little difference between the two job destruction rates, which are the source of worker job insecurity.

The authors found that only one-third of U.S. job destruction is accounted for by establishments that shrink by less than 25 percent over a year. Thus, the bulk of job destruction cannot be accommodated by normal rates of worker attrition resulting from retirements and quits. Most of the job destruction represents job loss from the point of view of workers. The authors also found that annual job destruction primarily reflects persistent establishment-level changes, so that the bulk of job destruction cannot be implemented by temporary layoff and recall. Most of the job destruction they measured reflects permanent job loss.

Baldwin, Dunne, and Haltiwanger (1994) also compared job destruction in Canada and the United States. They found that the Canadian and United States industry-level job destruction data are remarkably similar. Industries with high job destruction rates in Canada also have high rates in the United States, and similarly for industries with low job destruction rates. In addition, they found that the overall magnitudes of gross job flows in the two countries are similar. Further, they found that the time-series patterns of job destruction are similar in the two countries. In both countries, job destruction is much more cyclically volatile than job creation. This asymmetry, however, is more pronounced in the United States, giving some evidence that job insecurity is greater in the United States.

Wage Flexibility

Cousineau (1987) compared wage flexibility in Canada, the United States, and Japan. He found that wages in Canada and the United States are more rigid than in Japan, but that Canada has more flexible wages than the United States. He hypothesized that Canada has more flexible wages because it has a relatively small, open economy that is sensitive to international markets, in particular to the U.S. market. He found that wages in the sectors where exports are at least 25 percent of industry gross domestic product were highly positively correlated with U.S. output over the period from 1967 to 1984.

Employment Protection

An employment protection index has been created by the OECD based on the strength of the legal framework governing hiring and firing. Legal restrictions on hiring and firing may reduce job uncertainty for those workers having a job, but they also tend to reduce employment because of the inflexibility of the employment commitment by employers. Among 20 OECD countries, the United States ranked the lowest in terms of employment protection, followed by New Zealand and Canada (OECD 1994). Thus, in comparison with other OECD countries, Canada and the United States offer similar amounts of job protection through legal restrictions governing firing.

Advance notice is intended to reduce the risk associated with layoff by giving workers the opportunity to begin the search for a new job sooner, while still employed. In all Canadian jurisdictions, there are minimum requirements for notice of a dismissal without cause. Employers, however, may make wage payments in lieu of the notice period. Firing rules, working-time rules, short-time work arrangements, and regulations concerning atypical contracts are all aspects of Canadian employment protection legislation (den Broeder and Gelauff 1997).

In the United States, the Worker Adjustment and Retraining Notification Act of 1989 requires employers with 100 or more full-time employees to give 60 days' notice of a plant closing or a layoff that is planned to last at least six months and that involves at least one-third of the employer's workforce or 500 workers (whichever is less). Some evidence, however, indicates that this act has not increased the provision of advanced notice to displaced workers (Addison and Blackburn 1994).

Unemployment and Unemployment Compensation

Unemployment rates, which were nearly equal in the two countries in the 1950s and 1960s, were markedly higher in Canada in the 1980s and 1990s. Over the period of 1989–1994, the unemployment rate averaged 9.8 percent in Canada and 6.2 percent in the United States. In Canada, 24 percent of the labor force was unemployed at some point during 1993, compared with 15 percent of the U.S. labor force (Commission for Labor Cooperation 1997).

The unemployment rate has trended downwards in the United States. It peaked at 9.7 percent in 1982 and had fallen to less than 4.0 percent in the early 2000s.

The Canadian unemployment system is more generous, which may account for higher unemployment rates in Canada. The unemployment compensation system in Canada is more generous than the system in the United States primarily because of its less restrictive eligibility requirements and longer duration of benefits. Unemployment benefits are available for more than 40 weeks in Canada, as opposed to only 26 weeks in the United States, although the U.S. federal government often extends benefit durations in major recessions. Less restrictive eligibility rules imply that a larger share of unemployed workers are eligible for benefits in Canada than in the United States. Finally, the take-up rate among those eligible for benefits is higher in Canada. About half of unemployed workers in Canada in 1994 and 35 percent of unemployed workers in the United States from March 1995 to March 1996 received unemployment insurance benefits (Commission on Labor Cooperation 1997). For reasons poorly understood by policy analysts, many American workers fail to apply for the benefits available to them.

Unemployment insurance is not experience rated in Canada, while it is in the United States. The cost to Canadian employers of laying off workers is less than it is for American employers. Thus, the higher unemployment rates in Canada do not necessarily indicate greater income insecurity, taking into account social insurance.

THEORIES AS TO WHY JOB INSECURITY HAS INCREASED

Many theories have been proposed in the empirical studies as to why aspects of job insecurity have increased in Canada and the United States, at least through the early 1990s. We divide these theories into three groups: 1) macroeconomic theories, 2) employer-based (labor demand) theories, and 3) worker-based (labor supply) theories. Thirteen of the fourteen hypotheses present reasons why job and wage instability would be expected to increase. The first hypothesis presents a reason why they would be expected to decrease.

Macroeconomic or Economy-wide Theories

Declining macroeconomic instability

Some evidence indicates that the severity and possibly the duration of economic downturns have decreased. These decreases could be due to improved macroeconomic management of the economy, fortuitous changes in the severity of economic shocks, or other reasons not well understood.

Increased international trade

Both the United States and Canadian economies have increasingly opened to international trade. In 1995, Canadian exports accounted for 42 percent of GDP, up from 28 percent in 1988; U.S. exports accounted for 12 percent of GDP, up from 9 percent in 1988 (Commission for Labor Cooperation 1997).

International economic integration increases the exposure of an economy to external risk and to greater competition from foreign producers. Davis, Haltiwanger, and Schuh (1996) explored the effect of international trade on job destruction and creation. They found a high rate of gross job destruction in the United States among industries with a high import penetration ratio, as measured by imports as a percentage of imports plus domestic production. They speculated that this job destruction occurs because import-intensive manufacturing industries in the United States tend to pay relatively low wages and have relatively unskilled workforces. These types of industries tend to have higher rates of gross job destruction than do high-wage industries. To test this hypothesis, they examined the relationship between four-digit industry excess reallocation rates and measures of trade exposure. Excess job reallocation rates are measured as the difference between gross job reallocation (the sum of all plant-level gains and losses that occur over a time period) and the absolute value of net employment change. Regression analysis indicated that, after controlling for the level of wage rates in the industry, there was no significant relationship between excess job reallocation and measures of export or import intensity.

Davis, Haltiwanger, and Schuh (1996) focused on the demand of domestic and foreign consumers, and argued on theoretical grounds that the relationship between trade exposure and labor demand volatility is ambiguous. International trade exposes the U.S. economy to demand disturbances that originate in other economies, but it also reduces the importance of effects of domestic product demand disturbances on U.S. producers.

Considerable evidence shows that as imports become more competitive, domestic industry displacement rises (Kletzer 1998a, b; Haveman 1994; Addison, Fox, and Ruhm 1995). Haveman estimated that a 1 percent decline in industry import price from one year to the next is associated with a 1.62 percent increase in industry job displacements. For a group of import-competing industries, he found that a 1 percent decline in import price is associated with a 3.5 percent rise in displacements.

Decreased inflation

With the rapid inflation of the 1970s, firms could deal with competitive pressures by granting nominal wage increases below the rate of inflation, thereby reducing real labor costs without nominal wage cuts or layoffs. This form of adjustment was less available during the 1990s because of lower inflation.

Labor Demand

Increased competition

An overall increase in the level of competition, not just increases due to international trade, may have contributed to greater job insecurity. Increased competition has occurred in some industries due to deregulation. For example, the breakup of AT&T led to the entry of new firms and competition in an industry where jobs were once secure. The ending of price and other regulations has enhanced competition.

Duca (1998) argued that changes in how much competition an industry faces relative to others may explain why profit sharing has risen in some industries more than in others. He noted that the largest increases in profit sharing have occurred in sectors with greater foreign competition, such as in manufacturing, or in deregulated sectors, such as transportation.

Shift in bargaining power towards firms

The relatively slack labor market of the 1980s may have shifted bargaining power between firms and workers towards firms (Morissette 1996). The United States, however, has had low unemployment during the mid and late 1990s, shifting the balance in the opposite direction.

De-industrialization

The shift of jobs from the manufacturing sector to the service sector may be a factor in increasing job insecurity. Traditionally, jobs in the manufacturing sector have been more stable and secure than those in the service sector. This shift has occurred both in Canada and in the United States.

Technological change

The effect of rapid technological change on job insecurity likely differs between older and younger workers. Rapid technological change reduces the value of human capital of older workers, whose human capital was acquired in earlier years. For younger workers, however, rapid technological change is incorporated in their human capital because of their recent schooling and the greater investments in human capital that workers make at younger ages (Baumol and Wolff 1996).

Change in employers' philosophies

The United States and Canada have both seen a shift towards conservatism in political philosophies. There may have been a similar shift among employers away from the philosophy of paternalism and employer-provided social welfare and towards one of individual choice and individual responsibility.

Increased responsiveness of firms to economic conditions

Job insecurity can increase due to macroeconomic conditions or other factors affecting the firm's demand. It can also increase due a change in the response of the firm to those conditions. Such a change could be a result of other factors listed, such as greater competition, due to deregulation and increased international trade.

Labor Supply

Decreased unionism

Union members are likely to have more job security and stable wages than nonunionized workers because of job protection and multi-year wage contracts. Union members accounted for 17.6 percent of the workforce in 1993 but only 12.9 percent of the displaced workers over the period of 1993–1995 (Yakoboski 1997). Furthermore, job security under collective bargaining is tied to seniority, with older workers generally having greater seniority.

Unionization rates were comparable between Canada and the United States in the 1950s but were twice as high in Canada by 1990. A decline has also occurred in Canada, but it has been smaller and has been hidden in the overall statistics by the change in the labor force behavior of women. The overall percentage has stagnated, ranging from 31 percent to 33 percent between 1966 and 1993. The unionization rate fell from 38 percent to 35 percent for men, while it rose from 16 percent to 30 percent for women.

Both countries have seen a shift from the goods-producing sector, where unions are well established, to the service sector, where unions have recruitment problems. This shift has reduced union participation.

Between 1976 and 1992, employment declined in the Canadian goods sector, with its proportion of workers falling from 32 percent to 24 percent. As well, the proportion of unionized workers in that sector fell from 43 percent to 38 percent. In manufacturing, unionization fell from 43 percent to 33 percent. By contrast, total employment in the service sector grew from 68 percent to 76 percent of the workforce, and unionization in the service sector increased from 26 percent to 32 percent. The most heavily unionized part of the Canadian (and U.S.) economy is the public sector, where unionization rose from 69 percent in 1976 to 75 percent in 1993 (Galarneau 1996).

Verma and Thompson (1988) argued that Canadian and American managements responded differently to the market pressures of the 1980s. While many U.S. managers worked to develop a parallel non-union employment system, Canadian managers worked largely within collective bargaining. They concluded that managerial choice contributed to a decline of the collective bargaining system in the United States, while it had the opposite effect in Canada.

Decline in real income

Real incomes have declined for low-wage workers in the United States, though by exactly how much is unclear because the Consumer Price Index (CPI) has overstated inflation. Declining real incomes may have caused declining worker demand for employer-provided insurance.

The increase in two-earner families

The increase in two-earner families makes families better able to bear financial risks and thus more willing to take them, while the increase in divorce has had the opposite effect.

A demand by workers for increased flexibility

Some workers may have an increased demand for flexibility because of the changes in family structure. Working women may desire greater flexibility in an attempt to balance family and work responsibilities.

The age structure of the workforce

Some flexibility is provided employers by voluntary worker turnover and retirement. The greater voluntary worker turnover and retirement is, the less the risk of job insecurity. An aging workforce would seem to have a positive effect on job security because there would be greater flexibility due to retirements. A labor force with a high proportion of young workers would also be more flexible because there would be greater turnover. Thus, the demographic composition of the labor force may affect the extent of job risk individual workers face. A middle-aged worker would face less job insecurity in a firm with a high proportion of its employees being young or being near retirement. There may be an increase in job insecurity in the United States and Canada because the large baby boom cohort is middle aged, which is period of relatively low job turnover.

Summary

Each of the 14 hypotheses carries some supporting evidence. None is contradictory, and each could explain part of the changes that have occurred. The difficult task remains for empirical work to determine if some should be rejected and to determine the importance for those that remain.

CONCLUSIONS

Several measures suggest that job insecurity has increased in Canada and the United States, at least through the early 1990s. This trend appears to have reversed during the mid and late 1990s in the United States as unemployment rates reached 30-year lows. Even for that period, however, job insecurity was high relative to the unemployment rate. The demographic pattern of job insecurity has also changed. Job insecurity has increased for older workers in both countries, for whom the cost of insecurity is particularly high. Thus, the evidence is particularly strong that the cost of job insecurity has increased.

Thirteen hypotheses for an increase in job insecurity have been presented, although these should be interpreted as predicting the level of job insecurity relative to the unemployment rate and the level of aggregate demand for labor. The decline in unionism, for example, may be a factor in the decline in job security for middle- and lower-income workers. Greater international competition and greater competition due to deregulation may play a role in some industries. More rapid technological change may have increased job insecurity for older workers in some occupations. The low inflation rate may have increased real wage inflexibility. Greater macroeconomic stability may play a role in reducing job insecurity, but evidence suggests that much of job insecurity is idiosyncratic, not being related to macroeconomic shocks.

References

Addison, John T., and McKinley L. Blackburn. 1994. "The Worker Adjustment and Retraining Notification Act." *Journal of Economic Perspectives* 81: 181–190.

Addison, John T., Douglas A. Fox, and Christopher J. Ruhm. 1995. "Trade and Displacement in Manufacturing." *Monthly Labor Review* 118: 58–67.

Altonji, Joseph J., and John C. Ham. 1987. "The Collective Impact of Sectoral Shocks on Aggregate Fluctuations." In *Labor Market Adjustments in the Pacific Basin*, Peter T. Chinloy and Ernst W. Stromsdorfer, eds. Boston,: Kluwer-Nijhoff Publishing, pp. 161–201.

Andolfatto, D., and P. Gomme. 1996. "Unemployment Insurance and Labor-Market Activity in Canada." *Carnegie-Rochester Conference Series on Public Policy* 44(June): 47–82.

Baker, Michael, and Gary Solon. 1999. "Earnings Dynamics and Inequality among Canadian Men, 1976–1992: Evidence from Longitudinal Income Tax Records." Working paper no. 7370, National Bureau of Economic Research, Cambridge, Massachusetts.

Baldwin, John R., and M. Rafiquzzaman. 1996. "Restructuring in the Canadian Manufacturing Sector from 1970 to 1990: Industry and Regional Dimensions of Job Turnover." Analytical Studies Branch research paper no. 78, Statistics Canada, Ottawa.

Baldwin, John, Timothy Dunne, and John Haltiwanger. 1994. "A Comparison of Job Creation and Job Destruction in Canada and the United States." Working paper no. 4726, National Bureau of Economic Research, Cambridge, Massachusetts.

Baumol, William J., and Edward N. Wolff. 1996. "Protracted Frictional Unemployment as a Heavy Cost of Technical Progress." Working paper no. 179, Jerome Levy Economics Institute, Annandale-on-Hudson, New York.

Bernhardt, Annette, Martina Morris, Mark Hancock, and Marc Scott. 1999. "Job Instability and Wage Inequality: Preliminary Results from Two NLS Cohorts." *Journal of Labor Economics* 17(part 2): S65–S90.

Bordo, Michael D., Lars Jonung, and Michael Bergman. 1998. "Business Cycles Abroad." Paper presented at the conference, "Beyond Shocks: What Causes Business Cycles?" Federal Reserve Bank of Boston, June.

Borsjoly, Johanne, Gregg J. Duncan, and Timothy Smeeding. 1998. "The Shifting Incidence of Involuntary Job Losses from 1968–1992." *Industrial Relations* 37(April): 207–231.

den Broeder, Corina, and George M.M. Gelauff. 1997. "Between Commitment and Flexibility: Dutch Labour Market Regulations in International

Perspective." Presented at the conference, "Institutions, Markets and Economic Performance: Deregulation and its Consequences." Utrecht University, Utrecht, the Netherlands, December 11 and 12, 1997.

Calgary Herald. 1996. "Rules Penalize Employees Who Switch Pension Plans." February 18.

Carrington, William J. 1993. "Wage Losses for Displaced Workers: Is It Really the Firm that Matters?" *Journal of Human Resources* (Summer): 435–462.

Commission for Labor Cooperation, North American Agreement on Labor Cooperation. 1997. *North American Labor Markets: A Comparative Profile.* Lanham, Maryland: Bernan Press.

Corak, Miles. 1993. "The Duration of Unemployment during Boom and Bust." *Canadian Economic Observer,* Statistics Canada, September, pp. 4.1–4.20.

Cousineau, Jean-Michel. 1987. "The Impact of International Trade Shocks on Wage Adjustments in Canada." In *Labor Market Adjustments in the Pacific Basin,* Peter T. Chinloy and Ernst W. Stromsdorfer, eds. Boston: Kluwer-Nijhoff Publishing, pp. 61–78.

Davis, Steven J., John C. Haltiwanger, and Scott Schuh. 1996. *Job Creation and Destruction.* Cambridge, Massachusetts: The MIT Press.

Diebold, Francis X., David Neumark, and David Polsky. 1996. "Is Job Stability Declining in the United States Economy?" *Industrial and Labor Relations Review* 49(2): 348–352.

_____. 1997. "Job Stability in the United States." *Journal of Labor Economics* 15(2): 206–234.

Duca, John V. 1998. "The New Labor Paradigm: More Market-Responsive Rules of Work and Pay." *Southwest Economy* 3(May/June): 6–12.

Dunne, Timothy, Mark J. Roberts, and Larry Samuelson. 1989. "Plant Turnover and Gross Employment Flows in the U.S. Manufacturing Sector." *Journal of Labor Economics* 7: 48–71.

Employee Benefit Research Institute. 1999. "Male and Female Tenure Continues to Move in Opposite Directions." *Notes* 20(February): 1–4.

Farber, Henry. 1995. "Are Lifetime Jobs Disappearing? Job Duration in the United States, 1973–1993." Working paper no. 4859, National Bureau of Economic Research, Cambridge, Massachusetts.

_____. 1997. "The Changing Face of Job Loss in the United States, 1981–1993." *Brookings Papers on Economic Activity: Microeconomics* 2: 55–128.

_____. 1999. "Job Loss and Long-Term Employment in the U.S., 1981–1997." Unpublished paper, Princeton University, November 10, 1999.

Galarneau, Diane. 1996. "Unionized Workers." *Perspectives on Labour and Income* 8(Spring): 43–52.

Gardner, Jennifer. 1995. "Worker Displacement: A Decade of Change." *Monthly Labor Review* (April): 45–47.

Gordon, Robert J. 1982. "Why U.S. Wage and Employment Behavior Differs from that in Britain and Japan." *Economic Journal* 92(December): 13–44.

Gottschalk, Peter, and Robert Moffitt. 1994. "The Growth in Earnings Instability in the United States Labor Market." *Brookings Papers in Economic Activity* 2: 217–254.

_____. 1999. "Changes in Job Instability and Insecurity Using Monthly Survey Data." *Journal of Labor Economics* 17(part 2): S91–S126.

Green, David A., and W. Craig Riddell. 1997. "Job Durations in Canada: Is Long-Term Employment Declining?" In *Transition and Structural Change in the North American Labour Market*, Michael G. Abbott, Charles M. Beach, and Richard P. Chaykowski, eds. Kingston, Ontario: IRC Press.

Hall, Robert E. 1972. "Turnover in the Labor Force." *Brookings Papers on Economic Activity* 3: 709–756.

_____. 1982. "The Importance of Lifetime Jobs in the United States Economy." *American Economic Review* 72(September): 716–724.

Hamermesh, Daniel S., Joseph J. Cordes, and Robert S. Goldfarb. 1987. "Compensating Displaced Workers—Why, How Much, How?" In *Labor Market Adjustments in the Pacific Basin,* Peter T. Chinloy and Ernst W. Stromsdorfer, eds. Boston: Kluwer-Nijhoff Publishing, pp. 243–265.

Haveman, Jon D. 1994. *The Influence of Changing Trade Patterns on Displacements of Labor.* West Lafayette, Indiana: Purdue University, Krannenrt School of Management.

Hipple, Steven. 1999. "Worker Displacement in the Mid-1990s." *Monthly Labor Review* 122(July): 15–32.

Jacobsen, Louis S., Robert J. LaLonde, and Daniel G. Sullivan. 1993. "Earnings Losses of Displaced Workers." *American Economic Review* 83(September): 685–709.

Jaeger, David A., and Ann Huff Stevens. 1999. *Journal of Labor Economics* 17(Part 2): S1–S28.

Katz, Lawrence F. 1994. "Comment on Gottschalk and Moffitt." *Brookings Papers on Economic Activity* 2: 255–259.

Katz, Lawrence F., and Alan B. Krueger. 1991. "Changes in the Structure of Wages in the Public and Private Sectors." In *Research in Labor Economics: A Research Annual,* Vol. 12, Ronald G. Ehrenberg, ed. Greenwich, Connecticut: JAI Press.

Kletzer, Lori G. 1998a. "International Trade and Job Loss in U.S. Manufacturing, 1979–91." In *Imports, Exports, and the American Worker*, Susan M. Collins, ed. Washington, D.C.: The Brookings Institution.

Kletzer, Lori G. 1998b. "Job Displacement." *Journal of Economic Perspectives* 12(Winter): 115–136.

Kodrzycki, Yolanda K. 1996. "Laid-Off Workers in a Time of Structural Change." *New England Economic Review* (July/August), Federal Reserve Bank of Boston.

Lemieux, Thomas, and W. Bentley MacLeod. 1999. "Supply Side Hysteresis: The Case of the Canadian Unemployment Insurance System." Working paper no. 6732, National Bureau of Economic Research, Cambridge, Massachusetts.

Levy, Frank, and Richard J. Murnane. 1992. "U.S. Earnings Levels and Earnings Inequality: A Review of Recent Trends and Proposed Explanations." *Journal of Economic Literature* 30(September): 1333–1381.

Marcotte, Dave. 1994. "Evidence of a Decline in the Stability of Employment in the United States — 1976–1988." Center for Government Studies, Northern Illinois University, DeKalb, Illinois,

_____. 1995. "Declining job Stability: What We Know and What it Means." *Journal of Policy Analysis and Management* 14: 590–598.

McMurrer, Daniel P. 1996. *Job Security in the United States*. Washington, D.C.: The Urban Institute.

Morissette, R. 1996. "Why Has Inequality in Weekly Earnings Increased in Canada?" Analytical Studies Branch research paper no. 80, Statistics Canada, Ottawa.

Neumark, David, Daniel Polsky, and Daniel Hansen. 1999. "Has Job Stability Declined Yet: New Evidence for the 1990s." *Journal of Labor Economics* 17(Part 2): S29–S64.

OECD. 1994. *Jobs Study: Evidence and Explanations*. Paris: Organisation for Economic Co-operation and Development.

Polsky, D. 1996. "Changes in the Consequences of Job Separations in the U.S. Economy." Photocopy, University of Pennsylvania, Philadelphia.

Rose, Stephen. 1995. *Declining Job Security and the Professionalization of Opportunity*. Washington, D.C.: National Commission on Employment Policy.

Schmidt, Stefanie R. 1999. "Long-Run Trends in Workers' Beliefs about Their Own Job Security: Evidence from the General Social Survey." *Journal of Labor Economics* 17(Part 2): S127–S141.

Schmidt, Stefanie R., and Shirley V. Svorny. 1998. "Recent Trends in Job Security and Stability." *Journal of Labor Research* 19(Fall): 647–668.

Stewart, Jay. 1998. "Has Job Mobility Increased? Evidence from the Current Population Survey: 1975–1995." Unpublished manuscript, Bureau of Labor Statistics.

Swinnerton, Kenneth, and Howard Wial. 1995. "Is Job Stability Declining in the U.S. Economy?" *Industrial and Labor Relations Review* 48(2): 293–304.

Turner, John A. 1993. *Pension Policy for a Mobile Labor Force*. Kalamazoo, Michigan: W.E. Upjohn Institute for Employment Research.

U.S. Department of Labor. 1995a. "Displacement Spreads to Higher Paid Managers and Professionals." *Issues in Labor Statistics* 95–10 (August).

_____. 1995b. *Report on the American Workforce*. Washington, D.C.: U.S. Government Printing Office.

_____. 1999a. "Displaced Workers Summary." Labor force statistics from the Current Population Survey, Internet address: http://stats.bls.gov/news-rels.htm.

_____. 1999b. "Employee Tenure Summary." Labor force statistics from the Current Population Survey, Internet address: http://stats.bls.gov/news-rels.htm.

Ureta, Manuelita. 1992. "The Importance of Lifetime Jobs in the United States Economy, Revisited." *American Economic Review* 82(March): 322–335.

Valletta, Robert G. 1999. "Declining Job Security." *Journal of Labor Economics* 17(part 2): S170–S197.

Verma, Anil, and Mark Thompson. 1988. "Managerial Strategies in Canada and the U.S. in the 1980s." *Industrial Relations Research Association Series: Proceedings of the Forty-First Annual Meeting*, New York, December 28–30, pp. 257–264.

Watson, Mark W. 1994. "Business-Cycle Durations and Postwar Stabilizations of the United States Economy." *American Economic Review* 84(March): 24–46.

Yakoboski, Paul. 1997. "Worker Displacement, 1993–1995: Demographics and Implications." *EBRI Issue Brief* no. 186 (June).

3

Risk in Employment Arrangements

Sophie M. Korczyk

INTRODUCTION

This chapter explores the compensation-related risks that U.S. and Canadian employees can face due to the nature of their employment agreement and the policy issues such risks present.[1] Three types of employees are considered:

- Employees with jobs that are understood to be impermanent—these employees are called contingent employees.

- Employees with permanent jobs but not an ongoing relationship with a single, principal employer—the U.S. Department of Labor calls these arrangements alternative arrangements (Polivka 1996a). These employees include the self-employed, independent contractors, and temporary help and contract company workers, and may also be contingent.

- Part-time employees, defined in the United States as those who work less than 35 hours per week and in Canada as those working less than 30 hours per week. Part-time employees may also be contingent or alternative workers, but most are not.

Contingent, alternative, and part-time employment will be referred to in this chapter as "nonstandard" employment arrangements, as opposed to standard arrangements, under which employees have a full-time, continuing relationship with one employer.[2] Employees in the United States and Canada are considered in separate sections because of differences between the two countries in both data availability and institutional structures affecting compensation and benefits.

Why Worry about Nonstandard Employment?

The prevalence of nonstandard employment arrangements can signal many things about an economy and the operation of its labor markets. On one hand, the availability of such arrangements—and workers to fill them—would seem to provide evidence of an economy's flexibility and adaptability. Many nonstandard arrangements reflect technological advances, such as the increased availability and declining cost of computers, that make telecommuting or self-employment possible. Nonstandard arrangements can also allow workers newly entering or returning to the workforce to gain the skills and experience that can allow them to compete for permanent, full-time jobs, should they so desire. Such arrangements can therefore increase labor supply, income equality, productivity, and economic growth.

On the other hand, some observers believe that nonstandard employment can harm employee income security and productivity growth (see duRivage 1992; U.S. Department of Labor 1993). Nonstandard employees often earn less than similar standard employees, can lack many of the job protections available in standard arrangements and, in the United States, are less likely to have access to employer-provided health and pension coverage. Employers may not invest in training nonstandard employees because they do not expect to reap long-term benefits. Without training, employees are less productive and earn less. Employees in nonstandard employment arrangements may also be excluded from collective bargaining units (U.S. Department of Labor 1993). Some observers have thus questioned whether nonstandard employment arrangements increase income inequality.

NONSTANDARD EMPLOYEES IN THE UNITED STATES

Policy issues surrounding nonstandard employment depend significantly on how such employment is defined and measured. Until 1995, the nonstandard workforce was perceived to be large and growing rapidly. One estimate widely used before 1995 defined the contingent workforce to include temporary, part-time, self-employed (including business operators), and business services workers (Belous 1989).

Under this definition, contingent workers accounted for between 25 percent and 29 percent of the workforce during the 1980s and grew at a rate of 40–100 percent faster than the civilian workforce between 1980 and 1987.

The February 1995 Current Population Survey (CPS), a monthly sample survey of about 60,000 households conducted by the U.S. Bureau of the Census for the U.S. Bureau of Labor Statistics (U.S. BLS), changed the terms of debate over the nonstandard workforce. The CPS contained a special supplement aimed at estimating the number of workers in contingent jobs, defined as those structured to last only a limited period of time, and the number in certain alternative employment arrangements. That survey contained the first analytical definition of the contingent and alternative workforce as well as the first estimates of its size (U.S. Department of Labor 1995a). This definition is used in the U.S. discussion in this chapter. Under this definition, contingent workers accounted for 2.2–4.9 percent of the workforce and alternative workers—whether or not contingent—accounted for more than 9 percent.

The 1995 and 1997 CPS used three different definitions to identify contingent workers.

- Estimate 1 included wage and salary workers who had been in their jobs for 1 year or less and expected their jobs to last for an additional year or less. These workers accounted for 2.2 percent of total employment.

- Estimate 2 included the first group plus the self-employed and independent contractors who were in a similar situation with respect to expected job duration. This group included another 0.6 percent of the workforce.

- Estimate 3, which was the most inclusive, consisted of the first two groups plus any worker who believed his or her job was temporary or did not expect it to continue, regardless of past or expected time on the job. Adding these workers raised the contingent workforce to 4.9 percent of the total workforce, or 6.0 million persons.

These estimates suggest that fewer than 1 in 20 workers are contingent employees and fewer than 1 in 12 are alternative workers (Table

3.1). An additional 14 percent, or just over 1 in 7 are part-time workers who are neither contingent nor alternative.

These definitions are not easy to compare with those used before the CPS special survey (with its analytical definitions) was available. Belous (1989), for example, did not explicitly account for workers whose employment was subject to uncertainty. Thus, part-time workers would be contingent in his analysis whether or not their employment was subject to uncertainty (Table 3.2). In the CPS special survey, in contrast, whether or not a worker was classified as contingent would depend explicitly on the uncertainty attached to his or her employment.[3]

Table 3.1 Contingent and Alternative Employment Arrangements in the United States from February 1995 CPS Special Survey (% of total employment)

Category[a]	Estimate 1	Estimate 2	Estimate 3
Contingent	2.2	2.8	4.9
Alternative[b]			
On-call and day laborers	1.3	1.3	1.0
Temporary help agency workers	0.6	0.5	0.3
Independent contractors/self-employed	6.7	6.5	6.5
Workers provided by contract firms	0.5	0.5	0.4
Total alternative	9.1	8.8	8.2
Total part-time other than contingent or alternative	13.8	13.9	14.1
Total nonstandard	25.1	25.5	27.2
Total standard	74.9	74.5	72.8
All workers	100.0	100.0	100.0

SOURCE: Author's calculations based on U.S. Department of Labor (1995a).

[a] Many workers belong to more than one category, but each worker is counted only once in this table. Workers are counted first as contingent, then as alternative, then as part-time. The shares of alternative and part-time employment in this table therefore differ from those cited elsewhere in this chapter, where workers are allowed to belong to more than one category.

[b] Contingent employees with alternative work arrangements are not included. Workers who are both contingent and alternative are counted as contingent workers.

Table 3.2 Definitions of Contingent and Alternative Workers, 1989 and 1995–1997: A Concordance[a]

Belous (1989)	Current Population Survey (1995, 1997)
Contingent workers	
Temporary workers	May be contingent or not contingent
Part-time workers	May be contingent or not contingent
Self-employed workers[b]	May be contingent, alternative, or both
Business services workers	May be contingent or not contingent
	Contingent workers
Not assessed	Estimate 1: In their jobs 1 year or less and expecting to work an additional 1 year or less
Not assessed	Estimate 2: Those included in Estimate 1 plus self-employed and independent contractors in same situation
Not assessed	Estimate 3: Groups included in Estimates 1 and 2 plus workers not expecting their jobs to continue, regardless of past or expected time on the job
	Alternative arrangements
Not assessed	On-call and day laborers
Not assessed	Temporary help agency workers
All considered contingent	Independent contractors/self-employed
Not assessed	Workers provided by contract firms

[a] Each study's own definition of contingent and alternative workers is presented under the bold headings.
[b] Includes business operators.

Contingent Employees

Contingent and noncontingent workers identified in the 1995 CPS differed in several ways. Contingent workers were more than twice as likely as noncontingent workers to be young (ages 16 to 24) and somewhat more likely than noncontingent workers to be female and black. Young contingent workers were more likely (55 percent to 58 percent) than noncontingent workers (38 percent) to be enrolled in school.

Those not in school were somewhat less likely than noncontingent workers to have at least a high school diploma. Contingent workers were more likely than the workforce as a whole to be employed in the service sector, and two and one-half times as likely as the workforce as a whole to work part-time.

Part-time Employees

Part-time employees were the single largest group of nonstandard workers, accounting for 19.5 percent of the workforce in 1995, including contingent and alternative part-timers (U.S. Department of Labor 1995a). Part-time workers differ from full-time workers in several ways—they are younger, have less education, and are more likely to be female. On the other hand, black and Hispanic workers are slightly less likely than white workers to work part time.

Part-time workers earn less than full-time workers, not only because the former work fewer hours, but also because they are paid less per hour. When median hourly earnings of workers paid hourly rates are compared, part-time workers earn $0.62 for every $1.00 earned by full-time workers (Saltford and Snider 1994).

The risks faced by part-time workers depend not just on the hours they work, but also on their employment arrangements. Most part-time employees have standard work arrangements in all respects other than their hours worked; the CPS special survey found that nearly 90 percent of part-time workers were not contingent workers even under the broadened definition. But part-time workers were important among both contingent and alternative workers, accounting for 42.9–47.1 percent of the contingent workforce and 40.6 percent of the alternative workforce (U.S. Department of Labor 1995a).

Employees in Alternative Arrangements

Past estimates of the contingent workforce have included workers in alternative arrangements. These arrangements are not necessarily contingent under the definition used in the CPS special surveys. By defining contingent arrangements separately from alternative employment arrangements, the CPS highlights the differences in employment conditions faced by these two groups of workers. Most employees in alternative arrangements have the expectation of ongoing employment, although not necessarily with the same day-to-day employer.

Independent contractors

Independent contractors were the largest group of alternative employees and second largest group of nonstandard employees (after part-time workers) identified in the special survey, accounting for 6.7 percent of employment in 1995. The February 1995 special survey considered workers to be independent contractors if they said they worked as independent contractors or consultants, whether or not their business was incorporated. Independent contractors did not include self-employed persons who were business operators, such as shop owners or restaurateurs. This definition differs from the term "self-employed" as used in the basic CPS questionnaire, which includes business operators but excludes owners of incorporated businesses.

Independent contractors differed from other nonstandard employees in several ways. They were more likely to be 35 years old or older, white, and male. They were also more likely to be college graduates than any nonstandard employee group and than the workforce as a whole. Independent contractors were in fairly stable employment arrangements; just under 4 percent of independent contractors considered themselves contingent workers, a smaller proportion than in the workforce as a whole.

On-call workers and day laborers

On-call workers work only when needed. Examples include construction workers supplied by a union hiring hall or substitute teachers. Day laborers were defined as those who get work by waiting at a place where employers pick up people who work for a day. These workers accounted for 1.7 percent of total employment. Up to 38.1 percent of this group were contingent workers, depending on the definition of contingent workers used.

Younger workers and women were slightly overrepresented in this group in comparison with standard workers, while Hispanic workers were significantly overrepresented (12.5 percent vs. 8.6 percent).

Temporary help agency workers

Temporary help agency (THA) workers are under the direct or general supervision of an agency's client but on the payroll of the agency itself. Such workers represent a small share of the workforce, accounting for about 1 percent in 1995 (calculation based on U.S. Department of Labor 1995b). However, THA employment increased by 43 percent between 1989 and 1994, compared with an increase of 5 percent in total nonfarm employment over this period.

The majority of THA workers were contingent workers under the two more expansive definitions of contingent workers used in the February 1995 CPS. These workers were somewhat more likely than standard workers to be ages 20–34 and to be female; they were twice as likely as standard workers to be black. THA workers were also more likely than standard workers to lack a high school diploma.

Workers provided by contract firms

Contract workers were defined in the February 1995 CPS as those working for a contract company, usually for only one customer and at the customer's work site. Contract workers were the smallest group of employees with alternative arrangements, accounting for just over 0.5 percent of employment in 1995. Up to one in five contract workers considered themselves contingent workers, but most did not.

While on-call workers and THA workers were disproportionately female, contract workers were overwhelmingly male (71.5 percent compared with 52.8 percent of nonstandard workers). Contract workers were also better educated than both the standard workforce and all alternative workers other than independent contractors, with 60.8 percent reporting at least some college work. More than one in four contract workers were in professional specialty occupations, compared with about one in seven nonstandard workers.

Trends in Nonstandard Employment

New information such as that generated by the February 1995 CPS enhances understanding of workforce dynamics, but it also disrupts trend analyses because data under the new definition are not available for past periods. Of the categories of nonstandard employment considered in this chapter, longer term data are available only for part-time, self-employed, and temporary help agency workers. Flexible labor arrangements—including outsourcing, contracting out of various functions, temporary workers, and leasing entire workforces—can also be tracked over time. The February 1997 CPS special supplement also provides another observation point on the categories of workers identified in the 1995 survey (Cohany 1998; Hipple 1998).

Part-time workers

In February 1995, 19.5 percent of all workers (including all arrangements) worked part time (U.S. Department of Labor 1995a), up 3 percentage points from 1970. Part-time workers accounted for nearly 25 percent of the growth in the workforce between 1969 and 1993 (Saltford and Snider 1994). The voluntary component has remained fairly stable at 13 to 14 percent of the workforce (Saltford and Snider 1994). Involuntary part-time employment, however, has displayed both strong cyclical patterns and a long-term upward trend, increasing from 2.6 percent of the workforce in 1969 to 5.5 percent in 1993. Involuntary part-time employment thus seems to constitute a small but increasing source of economic risk for U.S. workers.

Self-employed workers

Many people believe that corporate and government downsizing has increased the level of self-employment. The CPS data on self-employment do not support this belief. Between 1967 and 1994, self-employment grew from 7.3 percent to 7.5 percent of the nonagricultural workforce (Bregger 1996). In agriculture, where self-employment has been more common, the proportion of self-employed declined from 51.9 percent to 48.3 percent over this period. When all industries are considered, self-employment declined from 9.6 percent to 8.7 percent of the workforce.[4]

Temporary help agency workers

In surveys of THA workers conducted in 1989 and 1994, the BLS found that employment grew far more rapidly in this industry as compared with the rest of the economy (U.S. Department of Labor 1995b). While total nonfarm employment grew by about 5 percent over this period, employment of THA workers grew by 43 percent. Put another way, while THA workers accounted for only 1 percent of the workforce, they accounted for over 6 percent of the growth in employment. White-collar jobs, once the majority of temporary help employment, were outpaced by growth in blue-collar jobs in THA employment.

Flexible labor arrangements

Changes in the prevalence of nonstandard employment arrangements are taking place against the backdrop of increased flexibility in labor arrangements or in the ways that firms purchase labor services. Many firms are moving toward flexible staffing, replacing direct hires with outsourcing, the contracting out of various functions, hiring temporary workers, and even leasing entire workforces (Clinton 1997). Such changes mean that some employment previously counted in the industry where it is performed is now counted in the services industry. As a result of such changes, employment in business services has grown by 6.9 percent annually since 1972, or about four times as rapidly as employment as a whole.

The growth in such market-mediated employment arrangements highlights the importance of definitions in understanding the contingent workforce. Contract, temporary, leased, or other employees may be "contingent" from the perspective of the firm for which their work is performed, but the CPS defines contingency from the perspective of the employee, not the employer. Thus, if these employees have the expectation of ongoing employment with the firm that hires them, they are not considered contingent under the CPS definition. Thus, while the majority of contingent employees work in the services sector, 97 percent of service-sector employees are not contingent under this definition (calculation based on U.S. Department of Labor 1995a).

Update from the February 1997 CPS

The February 1997 CPS special supplement shows mixed results on trends in contingent and alternative employment. Both the number and proportion of workers with contingent jobs fell between 1995 and 1997, with 4.4 percent of workers falling into the contingent category in 1997 (Hipple 1998), down from 4.9 percent in 1995. Overall, contingent workers in 1997 looked much like those in 1995—more were women, under age 25, enrolled in school, and employed part time than in the workforce as a whole in both years. Perhaps reflecting the strong economy of the mid 1990s, more contingent workers cited personal, rather than economic, reasons for their work arrangements, implying that more workers chose such arrangements voluntarily.

In contrast, the proportion of total employment accounted for by the four alternative arrangements surveyed in the CPS—on-call workers, THA workers, independent contractors, and contract company workers—was little changed (Cohany 1998). The characteristics of workers in these arrangements were also stable between the two surveys, with independent contractors continuing to dominate other alternative arrangements.

Employee Benefit Coverage among Nonstandard Employees

In the United States and Canada, work brings not just a paycheck but also a safety net in the form of employee benefits, whether legally mandated or voluntarily provided by employers.

Mandated benefits

Mandated benefits provided to employees in the United States include Social Security payroll taxes that finance old-age, disability, and survivor benefits as well as health care coverage in retirement; unemployment insurance contributions; and workers' compensation. Issues in providing mandated benefits to contingent and alternative workers depend on their employment arrangements.

Part-time workers are generally hired directly by the business for which they work. Their mandatory benefits are therefore provided in the same way as benefits provided to full-time workers.

Temporary and contract workers are generally covered by mandated benefits in much the same way as standard employees, but they may sometimes be able to look to more than one employer to satisfy an employer's obligations. This situation is sometimes referred to as "joint employment" or "co-employment" because two or more employers may have rights and duties with respect to the same employee (Lenz et al. 1998). For example, a THA bills its customer for the employee's wages and benefits, but the THA's obligation to pay the employee is not dependent on its being paid by the customer (Lenz et al. 1998). Likewise, while most states recognize THAs and employee leasing companies (firms that have an explicit co-employment relationship with the customer) as employers for purposes of unemployment insurance claims, customers in some states can be held jointly liable for unpaid unemployment insurance payroll taxes. On the other hand, the customer firm's co-employment status protects it from liability in workers' compensation cases since the exclusive remedy provisions of state workers' compensation laws typically extend to customers of temporary help firms.

What employees receive for the payroll taxes paid may be just as important to them as who pays the taxes. Employees must generally accumulate 40 quarters (10 years) with at least minimal covered earnings over their working careers to qualify for Social Security old-age, disability, or medical care benefits.[5] Many workers with short or intermittent work histories may therefore not be fully insured until fairly late in life.

Unemployment insurance carries benefit eligibility restrictions based on job tenure and earnings. These restrictions vary by state and may limit effective access to benefits for workers who change jobs frequently or work less than full time. Many states explicitly exclude casual workers from coverage.

Self-employed workers must make both the employer and the employee share of Social Security payroll tax contributions. They are excluded from unemployment insurance. They must purchase their own workers' compensation insurance if they wish to be covered.

Employer-provided benefits

Pensions and health care coverage are U.S. employers' largest benefits in monetary terms. One public policy concern about nonstandard employees in the United States is their lower rates of health and pension coverage. Coverage gaps raise equity concerns as all employees "pay" for tax incentives that support coverage available only to some.

Since most health and pension coverage is employment-related, coverage gaps also expose some employees to greater employment-related risks than others. Employees without pension coverage face greater risks of income loss resulting from disability or retirement. Employees without health care coverage risk inadequate health care, large financial losses, or both.

Pension coverage. Forty-eight percent of all workers were covered under an employer-sponsored pension plan in 1995 (Table 3.3).[6]

Table 3.3 Pension and Health Coverage by Type of Worker, 1995
(% of total employment)

| Employee category | Pension | | Health | | |
| | | | | Employer | |
	Covered[a]	Eligible	Total[b]	Covered[a]	Eligible
By contingent status					
Contingent workers	15	22	65	26	34
Noncontingent workers	50	57	83	62	74
All workers	48	54	82	61	72
By employment arrangement					
Alternative					
Independent contractors	35	NA[c]	73	34[d]	NA[c]
On-call workers and day laborers	19	25	64	17	27
Temporary help agency workers	3	7	45	7	23
Workers provided by contract firms	29	36	70	49	58
Standard	49	56	83	62	74
All workers	48	54	82	61	72
By hours worked					
Full time	56	63	84	71	82
Part time	16	21	72	17	32
All workers	48	54	82	61	72

SOURCE: Hipple and Stewart (1996a, 1996b).

[a] Includes employees covered by own employer at a main job or through another job or union. Employees who are eligible for coverage but who are not covered are not included.

[b] Includes employees covered as dependents of a covered worker or under other private coverage.

[c] Not applicable.

[d] Includes coverage purchased on own or through main job.

Most workers with pensions have full-time, long-term jobs. Half of noncontingent workers participated in employer pensions, compared with 15 percent of contingent workers (under the broadest definition).

There was considerable dispersion in coverage rates among workers in alternative arrangements. Only 3 percent of THA workers participated in employer pension plans, for example, but 35 percent of independent contractors had pension coverage, most through individual retirement accounts (IRAs) or Keogh plans.

Some nonstandard workers are explicitly considered in U.S. pension law. Under the Employee Retirement Security Act of 1974 (ERISA), employers may exclude part-time workers (those working less than 1,000 hours per year) from qualified pension plans. The Internal Revenue Code also requires that, under certain circumstances, customer firms count leased employees[7] to determine whether their pension plans meet the coverage tests that tax-qualified plans must meet. There are no other explicit legal requirements requiring the inclusion—or permitting the exclusion—of other nonstandard employees.

While the nature of the employment arrangement influenced pension participation significantly, whether an employee worked part time or full time was more important than the employment arrangement for all but THA workers. Fifty-six percent of all full-time workers participated in an employer pension plan, but only 16 percent of part-time workers did.

In recent years, researchers and policymakers have become interested in employees who are eligible to participate in employer benefit plans but decline to do so, sometimes because the cost of participating (contributions in pension plans or premiums in health plans) is too high. Workers in nonstandard employment arrangements are more likely to decline pension coverage for which they are eligible, but they do not tend to do this more often than employees in standard arrangements. Among standard employees, 7 percent decline pension coverage for which they are eligible (Table 3.3). Among nonstandard workers, this share ranges from a low of 4 percent (among THA workers) to a high of 7 percent (among contingent and contract workers). Nonstandard employees are thus quite "nonstandard" in their thinking about retirement income security.

Health care coverage. Nonstandard workers in the United States have significantly lower rates of health care coverage than workers in standard employment arrangements, but the difference in coverage by type of employment arrangement is not as large as in pensions. Among all employees, 82 percent reported health care coverage from some source, and 61 percent reported coverage through their employer at their main job or through another job or union (Table 3.3). As in the case of pension coverage, independent contractors displayed the highest health care coverage rate (73 percent) and THA workers the lowest (45 percent) among nonstandard employees.

However, when coverage is limited to that provided directly by the employer, workers provided by contract firms have the highest coverage rate among nonstandard employees (49 percent). Since coverage for independent contractors included that based on their main job or purchased on their own, it could be that people with coverage from another source—such as a spouse's employment—are more likely to strike out on their own.

As in the case of pension coverage, hours worked influenced the likelihood that an employee would be covered through his or her own employer. Among full-time workers, 71 percent were covered through their employer, compared with 17 percent among part-time workers.

As is also the case with pensions, a significant proportion of workers decline health care coverage; 16 percent of noncontingent workers and 24 percent of contingent workers decline coverage (Table 3.3). From the structure of the survey questions, it is clear that the workers are not declining coverage from their employer because they have it from another source.[8] Among standard employees, 12 percent without other coverage declined coverage for which they were eligible. Among nonstandard workers, however, only THA and part-time workers declined coverage at higher rates (16 percent and 15 percent, respectively). In the other nonstandard groups, the proportions declining coverage ranged from a low of 8 percent among contingent workers to a high of 10 percent among on-call workers and day laborers. Thus, while nonstandard employees are less likely than standard employees to be offered health care coverage by their employers, most are more likely than standard employees to accept coverage if they are not covered through another source.

NONSTANDARD EMPLOYEES IN CANADA[9]

Comparisons of nonstandard employment in the United States and Canada are limited by differences in data definitions. Information on contingent and alternative workers was not available for Canada using the February 1995 CPS definitions.

Detailed comparisons cannot, therefore, be made, but both countries have had broadly similar experience with nonstandard employment. In Canada, as in the United States, about one in three workers is in a nonstandard employment arrangement, if part-time employees are considered nonstandard (Table 3.4). The risks inherent in nonstandard employment differ significantly between the two countries, however.

Part-time Employment

Part-time employment is somewhat lower in Canada (15.0 percent) than in the United States (19.5 percent). While part-time employment as a share of the workforce has grown about 3 percentage points since the 1970s in both countries, cyclical patterns have been somewhat different. Part-time employment in the United States has tended to surge during recessions, declining after the recession has ended (Saltford and Snider 1994). In Canada, in contrast, recession-fueled surges in part-time employment seem to raise part-time employment permanently.

Another difference between part-time employment in the two countries is in employees' satisfaction with their situations. The pro-

Table 3.4 Trends in Nonstandard Employment in Canada: 1989–1994 (% of total employment)

Employee category	1989	1994
All nonstandard	30	33
Part time	15	15
Temporary	8	9
Own account (self-employed)	7	9
Standard	70	67
Total	100	100

SOURCE: Krahn (1995).

portion of Canadian part-time workers preferring full-time work tripled, rising from 12 percent to 36 percent, between 1976 and 1994. Involuntary part-time employment also increased in the United States over this period, although at a far smaller rate, from 23 percent of part-time workers in 1976 to 29 percent in 1993.

The increase in involuntary part-time work in Canada raises questions about why Canadian part-time workers were so much happier than their U.S. counterparts in the 1970s and why their unhappiness has escalated so rapidly since. Canadian part-time workers may have been happier in the 1970s because the overall part-time rate in Canada in 1976 was so much lower (11.0 percent) than it was in the United States (18.0 percent) that most Canadians who wanted full-time work may have been able to find it. In the years since, as the differential between the two countries has narrowed, involuntary workers appear to have accounted for most of the Canadian increase in part-time workers.

The increased prevalence of involuntary part-time work in both countries could mean that workers are bearing more risk. This risk would take the form of lost income and, for most U.S. employees, lost access to health care coverage because employers who offer coverage typically do not cover part-time employees. However, to understand the relationship between involuntary part-time work and risk it would be necessary to know what employees were doing before they became involuntary part-time workers. Those who were previously full-time workers are clearly bearing more risk as part-time workers. For those who were previously unemployed or out of the workforce, however, the situation is more ambiguous. If part-time work is an employee's best path into employment, then even involuntary part-time employment may represent a reduction, not an increase, in risk.

Self-employment

Self-employment is slightly more prevalent in Canada than in the United States. Independent contractors account for 6.7 percent of total employment in the United States, while the self-employed accounted for 9 percent of the Canadian workforce in 1994.[10]   Nonagricultural self-employment in the United States has been virtually level for nearly 30 years, while Canada has experienced steady long-term growth in self-employment.

Higher rates and growth of self-employment in Canada could reflect the added security provided to the self-employed by Canada's universal health care coverage system. In contrast, many self-employed persons in the United States have been able to obtain health care coverage only at a high cost, if at all, making self-employment less attractive.[11]

Temporary Employment

Trends in temporary employment in Canada and the United States are difficult to compare directly using available data. Between 1989 and 1994, the proportion of Canadian workers identifying themselves as temporary workers (in a job with a specified end date) grew from 8 percent to 9 percent of all working 15- to 64-year-olds (Krahn 1995). This definition appears to be narrower than the broadest CPS definition of contingent employment because it includes only those in a job with a specified end date and not those who merely do not expect that their job will continue. Based on this comparison, more Canadian than U.S. workers would seem to face employment-related uncertainty. However, as in the case of self-employment, the availability of universal health care coverage could make it more possible for Canadian workers to accept such uncertainty.

Flexible Work Arrangements

Work arrangements determine how work is performed and can encompass hours, location, and underlying contractual obligations between the employer and employee. Recent data on work arrangements in Canada provide further insights into the importance of nonstandard employment arrangements. The 1995 Survey of Work Arrangements, sponsored by Human Resources Development Canada and conducted by Statistics Canada, found that only one in three Canadians held a full-time, permanent, nine-to-five, Monday-to-Friday job with one employer (Human Resources Development Canada 1997). The remainder were in flexible arrangements, defined as temporary jobs, part-time jobs, jobs requiring more than 49 hours a week, job sharing, home-based or telework, flextime, weekend work, compressed work week, shift work, and self-employment.

Of the two-thirds with nonstandard time, place, or other arrangements, 46 percent—or 31.1 percent of all employees—were self-employed, worked part time, or were in temporary jobs. In short, these data confirm that some one in three Canadians work under a nonstandard employment arrangement.

Employee Benefit Coverage among Nonstandard Employees

Canadian employees may also receive both mandated and voluntary benefits from their employers. The structure of these benefits differs in some important respects from the United States, however.

Mandated benefits

Mandated benefits available to Canadian workers differ from those available in the United States. The old-age income support system favors employees with intermittent or short work histories. Much of the income support older Canadians receive is in the form of lump-sum old age security and the income-tested guaranteed income supplement, the values of which are independent of lifetime labor market earnings. The Canada Pension Plan (CPP)—the second-tier earnings-related old-age pension—is designed to replace about 25 percent of the average industrial wage. One contribution qualifies the worker for a benefit, but the CPP benefit can be low for workers without a full career since there is no minimum benefit.

Health care coverage for working-age people and their dependents—a voluntary benefit in the United States—is a mandatory, government-provided benefit in Canada (see Chapter 4).

Part-time, temporary, and contract workers are generally covered under both the unemployment insurance program (Employment Insurance, EI) and workers' compensation (see Chapter 7 for a discussion of workers' compensation provisions). As in the United States, self-employed persons and casual workers are generally excluded from EI and must purchase their own workers' compensation.

Employment insurance carries benefit eligibility restrictions as in the United States. Benefit eligibility is based on hours worked, a criterion that varies by locality and the unemployment rate in that locality. Most people must have worked between 420 and 700 hours in the previous 52 weeks to qualify for benefits, but the requirement for new entrants or re-entrants into the workforce is 910 hours. Thus, as in the United States, employees may be "covered" in the sense of having paid EI premiums, but may fail to qualify for benefits.

Employer-provided benefits

Employer pensions may be regulated at either the provincial or the federal level, which complicates generalizations about the treatment of nonstandard employees. However, the treatment of part-time employees in Ontario, the largest jurisdiction, illustrates the stance of Canadian pension law toward nonstandard employees. A part-time employee in the same job class as a full-time employee can become eligible for plan membership after 24 months of continuous service and must meet one of the following criteria: 1) 700 hours of work annually or 2) annual earnings of at least 35 percent of the maximum amount of earnings upon which CPP contributions are based ($37,400 in 1999) in each of two consecutive years before joining the plan.

Of the remaining provinces, all but one (Quebec) impose a service requirement for eligibility, and all impose an earnings-or-hours test for eligibility similar to the one used in Ontario. It is clear, therefore, that part-time employment is accommodated, but that only "committed" part-timers can expect to qualify for an employer-sponsored pension.

Coverage rates under employer-sponsored pension plans by type of worker were not available, but aggregate coverage rates for registered pension plans (RPPs) are somewhat lower than in the United States. In 1997, 42 percent of all paid workers participated in such plans (Statistics Canada 1998). Since these data do not include workers participating in pensions that are not RPPs[12] and hence are not covered by pension legislation, however, they are not comparable to pension coverage statistics for the United States.

ARE NONSTANDARD EMPLOYMENT ARRANGEMENTS INVOLUNTARY?

Several researchers have examined the prevalence of involuntary nonstandard employment arrangements (see, for example, U.S. Department of Labor 1995a; Polivka 1996b; Saltford and Snider 1994; Krahn

1995). An employee is considered in these studies to be working in an involuntary arrangement if he or she would prefer a different arrangement. Most part-time workers and independent contractors report that they prefer their current arrangements, but most THA and on-call workers do not (workers provided by contract firms were not asked this question in the CPS special survey due to the difficulties of providing meaningful answers to this question).

Involuntary employment arrangements raise both measurement and policy issues. Measurement issues concern the difficulty of determining why people do what they do and how they feel about it. For example, one part-time worker facing a constraint on work hours such as child care or transportation may classify himself as working part-time involuntarily, while another facing the same constraint may report the same decision as voluntary. Few surveys would be able to address this source of measurement error.

The policy issues raised by involuntary arrangements seem to depend on the nature of the barriers to the preferred type of employment. Involuntary arrangements that are undertaken for noneconomic reasons seem to represent personal choices with few policy implications. Involuntary arrangements that are undertaken because no alternatives are available (or because the employee believes none are available), on the other hand, could represent a form of hidden underemployment.

The February 1995 CPS allows some analysis of these questions. The survey asked both why respondents were in a contingent arrangement and what their preferred arrangement would be. Of those contingent workers who said they would prefer a noncontingent job, between 30 percent (under the narrowest definition of contingent workers) and 45 percent (under the broadest definition) cited personal reasons for accepting contingent employment (Polivka 1996b). Prominent personal reasons included being in school or training, flexibility of work schedule, and child care or other personal or family obligations. For many contingent workers, therefore, contingent work would seem to represent a personal choice.

The economic and public policy implications of involuntary arrangements also seem to depend on their duration. A temporary involuntary arrangement could be part of a job search or career change. Such an arrangement affords the employee a way to try out a new line of work, time to look for something different, or simply a way into the workforce, whether for the first time or after a period away.

A long-term, or even permanent, involuntary arrangement, in contrast, could suggest that even flexible, competitive labor markets such as those in Canada or the United States may fail to clear. Labor supply in any sub-market is fixed only in the short term; in the long term, workers can retrain, relocate, or both.

Evidence on the duration of nonstandard employment arrangements does not suggest pervasive labor market rigidities. Not surprisingly, the February 1995 CPS suggests that nonstandard employment arrangements, other than independent contracting,[13] are temporary for many employees. Contingent and alternative workers have dramatically shorter average job tenure than noncontingent workers, even when the definition of contingent workers is expanded to remove the one-year limit on actual and expected tenure. In 1995, 42 percent of noncontingent workers had held their current jobs for three years or less, but this proportion was 79 percent among contingent workers under the broadest definition. Likewise, 75 percent of workers in alternative arrangements other than independent contractors had less than three years on the job (author's calculations based on Polivka 1996b). It thus does not appear that most people in contingent or alternative arrangements are spending long periods of time in jobs that do not meet their needs. However, without a longitudinal survey that asks what happens to contingent workers after their current job ends, it is impossible to address this question conclusively.

The prior work history of many nonstandard workers provides further evidence that nonstandard employment is not a dead end. Other than on-call workers, the majority of contingent and alternative workers had been employed prior to their current jobs. However, while 25 percent of standard workers had been either out of the labor force or not employed prior to looking for their current job, this share was nearly 31.9 percent among all contingent and alternative workers, and 35.2 percent when independent contractors were excluded (author's calculations based on Polivka 1996b). And, even when they had previously been employed, more than half of contingent, on-call, and THA workers had spent a year or less in their previous jobs, compared with 40–42 percent of standard workers. In an economy where experience is valued and instability and job history gaps are sometimes viewed with suspicion by employers, nonstandard employment may serve as a way into the workforce for workers with little experience or spotty job histories.

POLICY ISSUES AND OPTIONS

New information on the nonstandard workforce raises several policy issues concerning pay-related risks these workers face.[14]

Who Is an Employee?

One issue concerns the adequacy of standard employee protections during periods of rapid evolution in work places and job descriptions. In particular, some employers may "convert" workers from employees to contractors or other arrangements to reduce their benefit costs. Such reductions can be substantial (U.S. Department of Labor 1999). Polivka (1996b) shows that while such conversions account for less than 1 percent of the U.S. workforce, they can account for a substantial proportion of workers in alternative arrangements.

Many people working in new places or arrangements—whether for the same or a new employer—may not realize that they remain common-law (standard) employees entitled to all the employment protections, such as payroll tax payments and other employee benefits, that cover such employees. Such employees may face more employment-related risks than is appropriate to their situation.

The U.S. Internal Revenue Service (IRS) has embarked on an enforcement program to improve protection for such employees. The IRS has issued new training materials for examiners and IRS representatives aimed at improving the process of determining whether workers are correctly classified (as employees or independent contractors) for tax and employee benefit purposes. The IRS has also implemented a classification settlement program in which agents have the authority to settle classification issues and work on prospective cures for employers who have misclassified workers.

Federal legislation has also been proposed in the United States to simplify the common law test for determining whether an individual is an employee or a contractor. Simplifying the test would make compliance easier for employers and monitoring easier for employees.

The definition of an employee is also being reviewed in some Canadian jurisdictions, also with an eye to improving employee protections (see Chapter 7).

Expanding Continuation Health Care Coverage for U.S. Part-time Workers [15]

Currently employers are only required to offer COBRA[16] coverage if they have 20 or more full-time equivalent employees on more than 50 percent of their typical business days. Under this approach, each part-time employee counts only as part of an employee. The law could be revised to count all employees equally. Since small firms employ a disproportionate share of part-time employees, such a change could expand the number of part-time employees able to keep their coverage in the event of a job loss.

Prohibiting the Exclusion of Part-time Workers from Pension Plans That Cover Full-time Workers

It would be possible to lower the hours threshold at which U.S. or Canadian employers may exclude employees from pension coverage or eliminate it entirely. Such a change would allow many part-time and short-service workers to accumulate pension credits. However, unless these workers have a substantial work history, such credits would probably not amount to substantial retirement income. Some Canadian jurisdictions are debating legislation to require or enhance the coverage of part-time workers under employer-sponsored pension plans.

Increasing the Access of Alternative Workers to Unemployment Insurance

Imposing federal eligibility standards for unemployment insurance in the United States could reduce state variability in employment protections for contingent workers (duRivage 1992).

Such changes would affect labor costs and employment. Examining such implications is beyond the scope of this chapter, but it is important to note that some nonstandard employment arrangements—

independent contracting is a prominent example—have challenged the enforcement capacity of regulators, particularly the IRS. Extending benefit eligibility to nonstandard workers without clear and enforceable definitions of who is such a worker could therefore increase public and private benefit costs without increasing risk protection for those most in need.

Devising policies to "deal with" contingent workers is also complicated by the fact that it is not clear how differences between standard and nonstandard workers should be interpreted. Are these differences problems to be addressed? Or do they demonstrate the ability of labor markets to respond to the varied needs of different types of workers and employers?[17]

CONCLUSIONS

Up to one in three U.S. and Canadian workers do not have a standard, full-time employment arrangement with a single employer. This share includes part-time workers, however, most of whom have standard employment arrangements in all respects other than hours worked. When part-time workers are excluded, fewer than 1 in 20 U.S. workers are contingent and fewer than 1 in 12 have alternative arrangements that may involve working intermittently or for a series of employers. These shares are far lower than many analysts have long believed.

Long-term trends in the nonstandard workforce are difficult to diagnose due to data limitations and changes in definitions, but trends in specific subgroups for which long-term data are available differ widely. The largest group of nonstandard workers in the United States—those working part time—has grown slightly as a share of the workforce over the past 25 years, while the second-largest group—the self-employed—has declined slightly. On the other hand, temporary help services employment, a very small component of the U.S. workforce, is growing at a rapid rate.

In contrast with the United States, part-time, temporary, and self-employed workers have all been increasing in Canada. Part-time employment and self-employment remain at levels comparable to those in the United States, but temporary employment seems to be more prevalent. Consequently, standard employment arrangements remain the norm in both countries, but nonstandard arrangements are changing in both importance and composition.

Numbers are not the only public policy concern regarding nonstandard workers, however. Some nonstandard workers work in such arrangements involuntarily, raising questions about the efficiency of the labor market's operation. Formal and informal job networks can provide information about employment opportunities, but employees without a permanent tie to a single employer may find it difficult to identify and make use of such networks. Lack of access to such networks can explain why some employees remain in employment arrangements that are not their first choice. On the other hand, most nonstandard workers in the United States (Canadian data were not available for this report) have much less time in their jobs than standard workers, suggesting that most people are not spending long periods of time in jobs they do not want.

Nonstandard workers also bear more employment-related risk than standard workers. In addition to the understood limits on the duration of their jobs, nonstandard workers have lower rates of retirement and health care coverage. Most also have lower hourly earnings than those in standard arrangements, although differences in age, education, and employment account for some of this gap.

Public policy efforts in the United States on behalf of nonstandard workers have largely focused on defining who is a standard worker and therefore eligible for the benefits and protections usually offered to such workers. A clear and enforceable definition of standard workers will make it possible to assess the need for expanded employment protection on the labor market frontier.

Notes

1. For a discussion of the legal treatment of other aspects of the terms and conditions of employment as they relate to nonstandard employees, see Lenz et al. (1998).
2. This definition does not include certain other types of nonstandard employment, such as multiple job-holding, that other authors have included in the category of nonstandard employment arrangements (see, for example, Commission for Labor Cooperation 1997). The range of nonstandard employment arrangements considered effects conclusions about their prevalence.

3. A revision of the CPS in 1994 further complicates comparisons over time.
4. As discussed above, the definition of independent contractors used in the February 1995 CPS is different from the basic CPS definition of self-employment. It is possible that independent contracting has displayed different trends over time from self-employment as a whole.
5. Special provisions apply to workers who become disabled or die before age 62.
6. Various surveys yield different results on pension coverage rates, reflecting differences in the populations surveyed and the structure of the pension questions (Doescher 1994).
7. While several tests apply, the most important factor distinguishing leased employees from employees in other employment arrangements is that the former work for the customer firm "substantially full-time," defined as at least 1,500 hours in a year.
8. Only those who first said they had no coverage from any source were then asked if their employer offered a plan to any of its workers and if they were eligible to participate if they chose.
9. This section is based on Krahn (1995).
10. An independent contractor as defined in the February 1995 CPS appears to be equivalent to the Canadian concept of "own-account self-employment," or self-employed with no paid employees (Krahn 1995).
11. The Health Insurance Portability and Accountability Act of 1996 is intended to increase the availability of health care coverage to many groups, including people losing or changing jobs, the self-employed, and small business owners. The Act does not address coverage costs, however, and thus might not make self-employment appreciably more feasible for most people.
12. For example, employers may contribute to a worker's registered retirement savings plan (RRSP), a savings instrument like U.S. individual retirement accounts (IRAs). Such contributions would not be considered "pension coverage" in Canada, although similar plans would be so considered in the United States.
13. The average job tenure of independent contractors was longer than that of all workers, regardless of type of arrangement.
14. Additional policy options can be found in U.S. Department of Labor (1993).
15. Since health care coverage is universal in Canada, this issue would not apply.
16. Under the Consolidated Omnibus Budget Resolution Act of 1995 (COBRA), certain former employees and their dependents are entitle to purchase coverage under employer plans after they are not longer eligible for coverage as employees or dependents. In most cases such coverage is only available for a limited period of time and is at the employee's expense unless the employer elects otherwise.
17. I owe the succinct expression of this point to an anonymous reviewer.

References

Belous, Richard S. 1989. "How Human Resource Systems Adjust to the Shift toward Contingent Workers." *Monthly Labor Review* 112(March): 7–12.

Bregger, John E. 1996. "Measuring Self-Employment in the United States." *Monthly Labor Review* 119(January/February): 3–9.

Clinton, Angela. 1997. "Flexible Labor: Restructuring the American Work Force." *Monthly Labor Review* 121(August): 3–17.

Cohany, Sharon R. 1998. "Workers in Alternative Employment Arrangements: A Second Look." *Monthly Labor Review* 121(November): 3–21.

Commission for Labor Cooperation, and North American Agreement on Labor Cooperation. 1997. *North American Labor Markets: A Comparative Profile.* Dallas, Texas: Secretariat of the Commission for Labor Cooperation.

Doescher, Tabitha A. 1994. "Are Pension Coverage Rates Declining?" In *Pension Coverage Issues for the '90s*, Richard P. Hinz, John A. Turner, and Phyllis A. Fernandez, eds. Washington, D.C.: U.S. Department of Labor.

duRivage, Virginia (ed.). 1992. *New Policies for the Part-Time and Contingent Workforce.* Armonk, New York: M.E. Sharpe.

Hipple, Steven. 1998. "Contingent Work: Results from the Second Survey." *Monthly Labor Review* 121(November): 22–35.

Hipple, Steven, and Jay Stewart. 1996a. "Earnings and Benefits of Contingent and Noncontingent Workers." *Monthly Labor Review* 119(October): 22–30.

_____. 1996b. "Earnings and Benefits of Workers in Alternative Arrangements." *Monthly Labor Review* 119(October): 46–54.

Human Resources Development Canada. 1997. *Applied Research Bulletin* 3(1): 5–7.

Krahn, Harvey. 1995. "Non-Standard Work on the Rise." *Perspectives* 7(Winter): 35–42.

Lenz, Edward A., Arlene F. Klinedinst, Elaine E. Herskowitz, and Deborah T. Garren. 1998. "Leasing Employees without Borrowing Problems: Developing Temporary Workforce Employment Issues." Presented at the Seventh Annual Employment Law Update, Virginia Bar Association, March 31, 1998.

Polivka, Anne. 1996a. "Contingent and Alternative Work Arrangements, Defined." *Monthly Labor Review* 119(October): 3–9.

_____. 1996b. "Into Contingent and Alternative Employment: By Choice?" *Monthly Labor Review* 119(October): 55–74.

Saltford, Nancy, and Sarah Snider. 1994. "Characteristics of the Part-Time Work Force: Analysis of the March 1993 Current Population Survey." *EBRI Issue Brief* 149(May).

Statistics Canada. 1998. *Pension Plans in Canada.* Catalogue #74-401-SPB. Ottawa: Statistics Canada.

U.S. Department of Labor. 1993. *Reinventing DOL.* Washington, D.C.: U.S. Department of Labor.

_____. 1995a. *Contingent and Alternative Employment Arrangements* (Report 900). Washington, D.C.: U.S. Department of Labor.

_____. 1995b. *Occupational Compensation Survey: Temporary Help Supply Services, United States and Selected Metropolitan Areas, November, 1994.* Washington, D.C.: U.S. Department of Labor.

_____. 1999. *Futurework: Trends and Challenges for Work in the 21st Century.* Washington, D.C.: U S. Department of Labor.

4

Health and Coverage At Risk

Robert B. Friedland
Laura Summer
Sophie M. Korczyk
Douglas E. Hyatt

INTRODUCTION

Over the past two decades, the financing and delivery of health care in the United States has undergone a dramatic transformation. The Canadian health care system is also changing and may, in the end, look more like the U.S. system than it does now. This chapter explains and compares the health care coverage risks for employees in the United States and Canada and examines policy options facing the health care systems in the two countries.

OVERVIEW OF THE U.S. HEALTH CARE SYSTEM

The transformation of the U.S. health care system has been primarily motivated by rising health care costs. Between 1988 and 1993 alone, for example, employers were faced with average annual premium increases of 12 percent (KPMG Peat Marwick LLP 1997). In response, employers attempted to control costs by making changes in benefits. Most workers now have an expanded role in the financing and delivery of their health care. The transformation of the health care system has also spurred federal and state legislative efforts to "protect the rights of patients."

Unlike the case in most industrialized nations, the U.S. health care system does not explicitly seek to provide health care coverage to everyone. There are a number of different sources of coverage and few national standards regarding coverage. People are not required to have coverage, nor are employers obligated to offer it. While private coverage is available to individuals, the relatively small individual private health insurance market covers only 5 percent of the population under the age of 65. Public health care coverage is limited to particular populations. As a consequence, not everyone has health care coverage, coverage is not uniform, and different systems for financing and delivering health care operate at the same time.

Employer Coverage

Most Americans—nearly 82 percent of the non-elderly population—have health care coverage, but over 18 percent or 43.1 million people do not (Employee Benefit Research Institute 1997a). Employers are the primary source of this coverage, providing coverage to 64 percent of the non-elderly population either directly or as a family member of a covered worker. In 1995, private health care coverage paid for 32 percent ($281.2 billion) of the nation's health care expenditures, which totaled $878.8 billion, on behalf of 70 percent of the population (U.S. Bureau of the Census 1997a, table 120; U.S. Department of Health and Human Services 1997a, table 1).

Employers take on differing roles for very different reasons. Some offer comprehensive coverage in an effort to attract and retain employees while others remain competitive even without offering health benefits. Some employers are not very involved with the design and administration of the health care coverage and essentially choose health plan options packaged by health plans or health insurers. Other employers operate their own plans and are in a position to make decisions about all aspects of the plan. Employers operate in different health care coverage markets and hence their ability to obtain and negotiate favorable coverage varies by the overall size of the employers and their size relative to the market in particular. Variation in employer involvement, flexibility, and options adds to the variation in financing that fragments and complicates health care delivery.

The Medicare Program

About 12 percent of the non-elderly population and 15 percent of the total population have public coverage, with Medicare and Medicaid being the two principal sources of public coverage (U.S. Department of Health and Human Services 1997b, table 1). Medicare is a federal program established in 1965 to help persons age 65 and older obtain and pay for medical care. Before Medicare, less than one-half of the elderly had hospital insurance and an even smaller proportion had coverage for outpatient care. In 1972, the program was extended to certain people under age 65: those with kidney failure and those receiving Social Security Disability Insurance (DI) benefits for at least two years. Currently, Medicare insures virtually all of the elderly in the United States. The program covers about 38 million people (33 million 65 and older and 5 million disabled) (U.S. Department of Health and Human Services 1997a, table 1).

The Medicare program has two parts. Part A covers inpatient hospital services, skilled nursing facility benefits, home health care, and hospice care. Part B covers physician and outpatient hospital services, clinical, diagnostic, and laboratory tests, durable medical equipment, and some additional supplies and services not covered under Part A.

Medicare is a major payer in the U.S. health care system. In 1996, Medicare expenditures were $203.1 billion or 20 percent of all health care expenditures (Levit et al. 1998). Medicare expenditures account for 22 percent of all inpatient hospital payments and 21 percent of all physician payments (U.S. Department of Health and Human Services 1997a, table 1). Medicare covers 44 percent of health care spending for the elderly overall, but a smaller share for the very old, who require more long-term outpatient prescription drugs, which Medicare does not cover (U.S. Bureau of the Census 1997a, table 153).

The Medicaid Program

Medicaid covers largely the very poor and the very sick. Other than low-income (but not poor) pregnant women and children, this program is not available to the vast majority of the working age population.[1]

The Medicaid program provides health and long-term care coverage to low-income individuals who meet certain eligibility requirements. The program is financed jointly by states and the federal government and administered by states. Broad federal guidelines are established for the program, but states have considerable discretion in establishing eligibility rules, determining the scope and depth of coverage, and setting payment rates for providers. While certain groups of individuals must be covered and a set of fairly comprehensive services must be provided, states have the option to expand eligibility to other groups and to provide a broader range of services. Consequently, the program is implemented differently in each state, and local health care markets are affected differently.

Medicaid was established in 1965 to cover participants in federally funded income maintenance programs for the poor (primarily dependent children and their mothers), the aged, and the disabled. Over time, program expansions have extended coverage to millions of people who are not in the welfare system and with the implementation of the new welfare program, Temporary Aid to Needy Families, enrollment in Medicaid is no longer automatic for families who receive cash assistance. In 1995, Medicaid covered 36.3 million people: 17.1 million children, 7.6 million adults in families, 4.1 million elderly persons, and 5.8 million blind and disabled persons (U.S. Department of Health and Human Services 1997a, table 72).

The federal government shares in the financing of Medicaid by matching state expenditures at varying rates. For health care benefits, the matching rate varies—from 50 percent to 83 percent—inversely with a state's per capita income. These federal matches are quite attractive and, over the years, states have effectively and creatively used the program to finance services that at one time were not a part of Medicaid. Despite state opposition to federal mandates, most states have voluntarily decided to provide most, if not all, the optional benefits covered under Medicaid.

With the program expansions, Medicaid has become a significant payer in the health care system. In 1996, Medicaid outlays were $131.1 billion or 14 percent of all health care expenditures (Levit et al. 1998). About 43 percent of the cost was financed by the federal government, the balance by states (Liska et al. 1997, table B-2). Medicaid accounts for 32 percent of all hospital and 20 percent of all physician payments (U.S. Department of Health and Human Services 1997a, tables 2–3). About 39 percent of all births are covered by Medicaid, as is health care for nearly 25 percent of children (Liska et al. 1997; Rowland 1995). Medicaid finances 47 percent of all nursing home care, provides health care coverage to 13 percent of the non-elderly population, and supplements Medicare for 3 percent of the elderly. Overall, half of all people living in poverty are assisted directly by Medicaid (Liska et al. 1997; Employee Benefit Research Institute 1997a).

HEALTH CARE COVERAGE IN THE UNITED STATES

The fragmented system of financing health care in the United States leaves many people uninsured or underinsured. The percentage of the non-elderly population without health care coverage has increased from 15 percent in 1987 to 18 percent in 1996 (Employee Benefit Research Institute 1997a,b). This change is due, in part, to a decline in employer-provided coverage, although that decline has been offset somewhat by an increase in the proportion of the population with publicly funded coverage.

Some Groups are More Likely to Have Health Care Coverage

Coverage rates vary widely across demographic groups. Children are more likely than non-elderly adults to be insured. Expansions in the Medicaid program have played a significant role in increasing the proportion of children with health care coverage. The age group least likely to have care coverage is young adults, ages 19–24 (U.S. Department of Health and Human Services 1997b, table 1).

There are significant differences in coverage patterns for racial and ethnic groups. Among the non-elderly, Hispanics are most likely to be uninsured (34 percent), followed by blacks (23 percent). A much smaller proportion of whites (13 percent) is uninsured (U.S. Department of Health and Human Services 1997b, table 2). Income is another factor that affects coverage. Despite the existence of Medicaid, about 34 percent of the non-elderly poor have no health care coverage compared with 18 percent of the non-elderly population as a whole (U.S. Bureau of the Census 1997b).

Married individuals are more likely to be insured than individuals who have never been married or who are no longer married (U.S. Department of Health and Human Services 1997b, table 2). It appears that education has an impact on coverage status; among adults, the likelihood of being uninsured declines as the level of education rises (Bennefield 1997).

Coverage is higher in metropolitan areas and in the Northeast and Midwest regions of the country. Coverage is lower outside metropolitan areas, in the West, and in the South (U.S. Department of Health and Human Services 1997b, table 2).

The coverage status of workers

Employment status remains the most important factor related to health care coverage. Some 82 percent of employed individuals have coverage, compared with 74 percent of unemployed individuals (U.S. Department of Health and Human Services 1997b, table 2). The health care coverage status of workers is discussed in more detail below.

Almost one-fifth (18.4 percent) of working adults are uninsured and a similar percentage of all persons in families with working adults (18.5 percent) have no coverage (U.S. Department of Health and Human Services 1997b, table 2). Working adults account for half (50.4 percent) of all the uninsured in the United States and almost 87 percent of the uninsured population lives in households with a working adult.

Employment grew by 15 percent and unemployment rates declined by 20 percent between 1987 and 1997 (Executive Office of the President 1999), yet employment-related health care coverage decreased from 69 percent of the non-elderly population in 1987 to 64 percent in 1997 (Figure 4.1). Over the same period, the percentage of full-time workers without coverage increased from 13 percent to nearly 15 percent (Figure 4.1; Employee Benefit Research Institute 1997a, figure 6). Yet, despite the rise in costs and decline in coverage, the number of employers offering coverage has increased. These seemingly inconsistent trends indicate that the employer-based coverage system is not simple.

Age. Younger workers are most likely to lack health care coverage. More than one-third (36 percent) of young adults aged 19–24 have no coverage. Workers aged 19–24 account for 12 percent of the workforce but 23 percent of uninsured workers. The 25- to 29-year-old group also has low coverage rates—nearly one in four (23 percent) lacks coverage.

Figure 4.1 Employment-Based Health Care Coverage

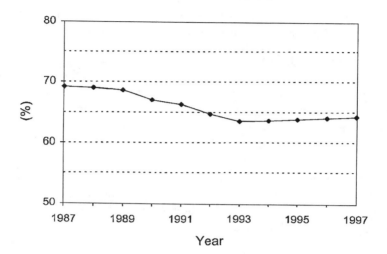

In general, coverage rates increase with age, and the increase is due to increases in employment-related coverage. Just over half of all 19- to 24-year-olds (53 percent) have employment-related coverage, that is, they are covered through their own or a relative's job. By contrast, more than three-quarters of 45- to 54-year-olds (79 percent) have coverage. After age 55, employment-related coverage decreases slightly, but more than three-quarters (76 percent) of adults aged 55–64 still have employment-related coverage (U.S. Department of Health and Human Services 1997c, table 2).

Gender. Working women have higher levels of employment-related coverage (84 percent) than working men (79 percent) (U.S. Department of Health and Human Services 1997c, table 2). It is interesting to note, however, that working women are less likely to have employment-related health care coverage in their own names (40 percent) than are working men (55 percent) (U.S. Department of Health and Human Services 1997c, p. 2). In addition to receiving coverage from their own employers, some working women are covered as dependents of working men. The proportion of non-elderly men with employment-based coverage in their own name decreased from 59 percent in 1987 to 55 percent in 1995. Among women, the percentage increased from 37 percent to 40 percent during the same period, but direct coverage for women still lags behind direct coverage for men (Employee Benefit Research Institute 1997a, figure 18).

Ethnic group. Coverage rates are much higher for white workers than they are for minority workers. Hispanics have the lowest rates, with just 55 percent of the population covered. Among blacks, coverage is 66 percent, compared with 77 percent of whites. Within racial and ethnic groups, women are more likely to have employment-related coverage than men. The group with the lowest rate of coverage is Hispanic males; more than two in five (44 percent) lack coverage. By comparison, 30 percent of black male workers and 17 percent of white male workers are uninsured. While Hispanic males account for just 6 percent of workers aged 16–64, they account for 13 percent of uninsured workers (table 2 in U.S. Department of Health and Human Services 1997c).

Hours worked. Part-time workers are less likely than full-time workers to have employment-related coverage. In 1995, some 63 percent of full-time workers aged 18–64 had employment-based coverage in their own name, more than three times the coverage rate for part-time workers (20 percent) (U.S. Department of Health and Human Services 1997c, figure 4). Part-time workers are also more likely than their full-time colleagues to be uninsured. One in four part-time workers and 17 percent of full-time workers are uninsured (U.S. Department of Health and Human Services 1997c, figure 6).

Overall, 58 percent of part-time workers aged 16 and older have employment-related coverage. Older workers, aged 55–64, have the highest rates of coverage. Some 64 percent of older part-time workers are covered either as workers or as dependents of workers (Employee Benefit Research Institute 1997c, table 1).

Male part-time workers are less likely to have employment-related coverage than female part-time workers (52 percent vs. 61 percent). There is little difference between the genders in terms of coverage under their own name, but female part-time workers are more likely to be covered as dependents (Employee Benefit Research Institute 1997c, table 1).

Coverage for part-time workers increased from 17 percent to 20 percent between 1987 and 1995. The percentage of part-time workers without coverage was higher (22.4 percent) in 1995 than it was in 1987 (19.7 percent), but the 1995 rate was lower than the highest rate of uninsured part-time workers (23.7 percent) reported in 1992 (Employee Benefit Research Institute 1997a, figure 6).

Self-employment. Only half of self-employed workers have employment-related coverage, while more than three quarters (77.1 percent) of workers who are not self-employed have insurance (U.S. Department of Health and Human Services 1997, table 3). This difference may reflect U.S. tax policy, which allows self-employed workers to deduct only 30 percent of what they spend on health care coverage, while employer contributions to coverage made on behalf of wage earners are fully deductible from taxable income.

Lower rates of insurance for the self-employed, however, may also be related to the fact that the self-employed are more likely to work in small firms and therefore may face higher premiums. Fewer than half of the self-employed who work alone (45.4 percent) have employment-related coverage, compared with 72.7 percent in businesses with 10 or more workers.

As with all workers, coverage rates for self-employed workers aged 18–64 decreased from 27.9 percent in 1987 to 25.4 in 1995, although there was some fluctuation over the years (Employee Benefit Research Institute 1997a, table 4).

Employer size. Workers and their dependents without coverage are more likely to work for smaller firms in industries that have not traditionally needed to offer coverage. The proportion of workers with employment-related coverage increases with the size of the firm. In firms with fewer than 10 workers, 58.8 percent of wage earners had employment-related coverage. In firms with 500 or more workers, 91 percent of wage earners had employment-related coverage. Conversely, the proportion of uninsured wage earners decreases as firm size increases. Almost one-third of wage earners (30.4 percent) in firms with fewer than 10 workers were uninsured compared with just 6.7 percent in the largest firms, those with 500 or more workers (U.S. Department of Health and Human Services 1997c, table 3). About

15.4 percent of workers are employed in firms with fewer than 10 workers, but they account for 25.4 percent of uninsured workers (U.S. Department of Health and Human Services 1997c, table 5).

In the 1990s, it became more common for small firms to offer coverage. Among all firms with fewer than 200 employees, coverage was offered by 46 percent in 1989 and 49 percent in 1996. The percentage of employees enrolled in plans offered by small firms declined, however, during the same period from 72 percent in 1989 to 66 percent in 1996. The likely reason for the decline is that workers cannot afford to pay for coverage. The average monthly contribution for workers in small firms increased from $34 in 1988 to $175 in 1996 (Ginsburg, Gabel, and Hunt 1998).

Workers in all firms were more likely to be uninsured in 1995 than in 1987. Over time, there has been a decrease in the proportion of workers in large firms who have coverage. Some 73.3 percent of workers in firms with 500 or more workers had coverage in 1987, compared with 68.1 percent in 1995. The coverage rate for smaller firms remained about the same from 1987 to 1995 (Employee Benefit Research Institute 1997a, figure 7).

Wages. As they compete to attract and retain skilled workers, firms must offer attractive benefit packages. Workers who earn more money are therefore more likely than workers at the lower end of the wage scale to have coverage. Fewer than half of the lowest wage earners (43.3 percent) have employment-related coverage, but 95.5 percent of wage earners at the highest end of the scale have employment-related coverage. It is not surprising, then, that more than one-third of the lowest wage workers (37.8 percent) have no coverage, compared with just 2.9 percent of the highest wage workers. Even so, between 1987 and 1995, the highest income group had the largest decrease in the percentage of employment-related coverage. Some 86.5 percent of workers with earnings of $40,000 or more had coverage in 1987, compared with 81.6 percent in 1995 (Employee Benefit Research Institute 1997a, figure 9).

Industry. Some industries—agriculture, personal services, construction, retail, business repair services, and recreation—are substantially less likely to provide coverage. Some of these categories represent the sectors of the economy in which employment opportunities are growing the fastest. Coverage is more likely to be provided in sectors in which employment opportunities have been growing slowly and even declining. These include mining, manufacturing, government, finance, insurance, and real estate, as well as transportation, utilities, and the communications industry. Some of those trends may be tied to the past. For example, 92.8 percent of unionized workers but 71 percent of nonunionized workers are covered by employment-related insurance.

A Lack of Coverage Limits Access to Care

Coverage matters; access to health care services is severely limited for the uninsured. More than one-quarter of people without any coverage (27 percent) report that they had difficulties or delays in obtaining health care when they needed it. The rate is more than twice as high as for those with public coverage (12 percent) and almost four times as high as people with private coverage (7 percent).

The cost of health care prevents some families from getting the services they need. More than one-third of privately insured families (37 percent) and close to half of publicly insured families (46 percent) say they have difficulties obtaining health care services because they cannot afford the care despite having coverage. The problem is greatest for uninsured families, however, with 87 percent reporting that they cannot afford care (U.S. Department of Health and Human Services 1997d, table 1).

Another measure of access to care is whether people have a usual source of health care. The uninsured are much more likely to lack such a source than those with coverage. Some 38 percent of uninsured people say they do not have a usual source of health care compared with 15 percent of those with private coverage and 13 percent of those with public insurance (U.S. Department of Health and Human Services 1997d, table 1). A national survey of coverage conducted in 1997 found that uninsured adults were four times as likely as those who were continuously insured not to have received needed medical care or to have not filled a prescription in the past year (Kaiser Family Foundation and The Commonwealth Fund 1997).

Ratings related to the quality of care also vary by coverage status. In a recent survey of low-income adults in five states, almost one-third of the uninsured reported that the services they received had been fair or poor, compared with 18 percent of those with Medicaid and 17 percent of those with private insurance (Schoen et al. 1997).

The gulf in access to care is certainly greatest between those with coverage and those without, but having an insurance card is not necessarily sufficient to ensure access to health care since coverage varies dramatically in its scope and depth. Health insurance policies range from those that provide comprehensive coverage for all health care services related to illness and preventive care to those that only provide coverage for catastrophic care. Most policies limit coverage by excluding some services and limiting the amount of certain services that will be covered. Also, large deductibles or copayments may serve to limit the amount of care that people seek.

While Medicare provides good coverage for the elderly, it appears that people who supplement their Medicare coverage, and therefore have more comprehensive coverage, have better access to care. Among the elderly, some 11.9 percent of those covered only by Medicare lack a usual source of health care compared with 7.7 percent of elderly people covered by other public or private insurance in addition to Medicare (U.S. Department of Health and Human Services 1997d, table 1).

Increasing Risk in the Coverage Market

The coverage most employers offer today is different from what was available in the past.

Coverage pays less

For those who still have coverage, the coverage is less comprehensive than it has been in the past. Conventional plans used to pay the full cost or close to the full cost of health care. Throughout the 1980s, however, employers moved away from health insurance policies that offer first-dollar coverage for any provider. Instead, employers are frequently required to meet certain deductibles before insurers will pay for care. In addition, requirements for copayments for certain services have become much more common. Also, health insurance policies with limits on the maximum amount that will be paid over the course of a person's life have become more common (Employee Benefit Research Institute 1997d, tables 30.5 and 30.8).

Employers pay less

Employers have moved away from full coverage of premiums, leaving to some employees a clearer choice between more direct compensation or more benefits. In 1983, almost all full-time employees in medium and large firms (96 percent) participated in health insurance plans. By 1993, participation had dropped to 82 percent. At the same time, the percentage of medium and large employers that fully financed health insurance for individual employees decreased substantially from 73 percent in 1981 to 37 percent in 1993. Similarly, the percentage that fully financed family coverage dropped from 51 percent in 1981 to 21 percent in 1993 (Employee Benefit Research Institute 1997d, tables 30.5 and 30.8).

The proportion of premiums paid by employees has also increased. In 1988, employees in small and large firms paid 34 percent and 29 percent, respectively, of premiums for family coverage. By 1996, payments for premiums had increased to 44 percent for employees in small firms and 30 percent for employees in large firms (Figures 4.2A and 4.2B).

It is likely that the financial burdens for individuals and families associated with health insurance coverage have led to an increase in the percentage of employees who turn down coverage. The high cost of health insurance premiums and deductibles may cause some employees to decline coverage even when it is available from employers. In firms that offer health insurance benefits, the percentage of employees enrolled has declined from 72 percent in 1989 to 66 percent in 1996 for small firms and from 73 percent in 1989 to 67 percent in 1996 for large firms (Ginsburg, Gabel, and Hunt 1998).

Firms of all sizes increasingly have made an effort to control health care costs by self-insuring. Rather than buying coverage, employers set money aside and then use the funds to pay benefits. The percentage of employers self-funding indemnity plans grew from 19 percent in 1993 to 30 percent in 1996, and the percentage of self-funding preferred-provider plans grew from 6 percent in 1993 to 26 percent in 1996 (tables 28.1 and 28.2 in Employee Benefit Research Institute 1997d). Self-insurance can reduce employer health care costs by bypassing state mandates to cover certain providers or services. But, to

Figure 4.2A   Premium Shares by Type of Coverage in Smaller Firms, 1988 and 1996

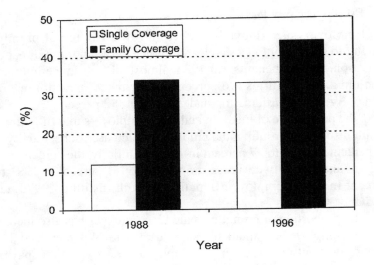

Figure 4.2B   Premium Shares by Type of Coverage in Larger Firms, 1988 and 1996

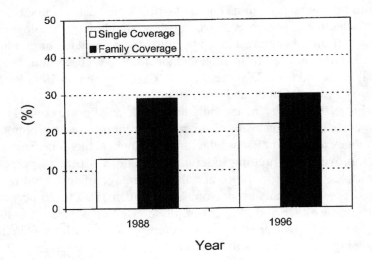

the extent that employers turn to self-insurance for this purpose, the value of health care coverage to employees can decline.

Family coverage is less common

The decline in family coverage certainly is consistent with employer efforts to limit health care expenditures, but it also reflects the fact that it is more likely that both spouses are working, increasing a couple's potential coverage sources. Between 1980 and 1996, the labor force participation rate for married women increased from 50 percent to 61 percent (U.S. Bureau of the Census 1997a, table 630).

Employers are shifting costs to both employees and other employers by encouraging employees to obtain coverage through a working spouse's health plan. However, according to interviews by Silow-Carroll et al. (1995), employers do not want to subsidize health insurance premiums of employees of other firms. Others noted that under the current system, it makes the most sense to ask business to continue covering families even if some businesses are carrying a disproportionate share of the burden. Only one respondent favored paying an extra amount to regional alliances for family coverage cases, and some small employers said the uninsured should be "made to go out and work for health benefits like the rest of us."

Employers are more likely to offer managed care plans

During the 1990s, employers have moved more aggressively into managed care plans in an effort to control costs. Managed care plans include health maintenance organizations as well as less restrictive arrangements, such as preferred-provider organizations and point of service plans. All require or encourage enrollees to use specific groups or networks of health care providers.

In 1997, managed care plans comprised 81 percent of the health insurance market, up from 29 percent in 1988. One reason for this large shift is that fewer employers provide the option of a conventional plan. In 1997, only 51 percent of workers could choose a conventional plan, compared with 89 percent in 1988 (KPMG Peat Marwick LLP 1997).

Initially, managed care was a large-employer movement, but recent growth in managed care enrollment reflects a shift among small firms as well. Some employers have made the change because costs are lower in managed care plans, and some have been forced to change because indemnity plans are not available.

From a consumer's perspective, the movement towards managed care plans can be advantageous because it eliminates some requirements for deductibles and/or copayments. Coordination among providers may also be easier in managed care plans, improving patients' health outcomes, but managed care may pose other dilemmas due to stricter limits on benefits and rules related to available services, provider choice, and prescription drugs. Recent interest on the part of policymakers in the extent to which managed care plans restrict services indicates that the manner in which the plans operate will continue to evolve.

Risks Associated with Employer-provided Coverage

As the health insurance system in the United States has evolved, and particularly as more firms have adopted managed care plans, the risks associated with providing and using health insurance have increased.

Risks for employers

The anticipation and reaction of both real and perceived risks by employers affect the health insurance risks faced by employees. Employers face both financial and administrative risks.

The cost of coverage poses financial risks. Employer-financed health care expenditures are increasing. As a percentage of total compensation, employer-financed health insurance has increased relatively steadily from 1.1 percent in 1960, to 4.4 percent in 1980, to 7.6 percent in 1994 (Employee Benefit Research Institute 1997d, table 34.1). In 1960, health benefits accounted for 14.3 percent of all employer benefit spending. By 1994, 40.8 percent of benefit spending was for health benefits (Employee Benefit Research Institute 1997d, table 2.2).

In the late 1990s, increases in health plan premiums were quite low relative to previous years. The increase from spring 1996 to spring 1997 was just 2.1 percent (KPMG Peat Marwick LLP 1997). Based on these figures, many employers believed they had effectively contained health care costs. There are indications, however, that this may not be the case. While the shift to managed care can achieve savings, most of the savings so far has come from one-time changes. Health care inflation both within health plans and outside of health plans has been essentially the same, although there is some evidence to suggest that the overall cost increases in communities with substantially larger managed care penetration are less (Price Waterhouse LLP 1995).

While the more aggressive firms may succeed in lowering their own costs, they do not necessarily lower the overall cost of health care, just the distribution of those costs among payers. As a result, even if some firms make every effort to keep their own costs low, they may still see their health care costs rise because they cannot control the broader market.

The level of risk posed by health care costs varies for employers. For firms that do not already offer health insurance—generally smaller or newer firms—the transition costs associated with providing coverage represent a major expense. If they decide to offer insurance, they might have to forego other opportunities. However, if they need to offer health benefits to attract or retain specific employees, the cost may seem less onerous.

For most established businesses, it is not the cost of health care per se that is problematic. It is routinely viewed as part of the cost of labor. Unanticipated increases in health care costs pose risks, however. Unlike other inputs into the cost of business, this component of labor costs is not very predictable and there is no futures market to help stabilize unanticipated costs. When health care costs exceed budgets, employers must cut other costs, delay hiring new employees, or delay making capital improvements.

There is some disagreement about how much of the increased health care costs employers absorb and how much is passed on to employees, passed forward to consumers, or passed back to stockholders. In the short-term, employers must pay the cost. Yet, many employers argue that product prices are higher than those of their international competitors because of the higher cost of health care. However, there is evidence that over time, employers adjust wages to compensate for increases in the cost of health care (Silow-Carroll et al. 1995). In all likelihood, cost increases are passed in every direction, but the degree and speed to which the unexpected cost increases are absorbed will depend on the market conditions in which an employer incurs them.

Employers have new responsibilities associated with administering plans. In addition to paying for health insurance, employers must learn about various plans to determine which plans best fit their needs and the needs of their employees. If they offer more than one plan—as most large firms do—they must provide information to help employees choose plans. With the advent of managed care, employers are expected to help their employees understand various rules associated with the plans, such as the fact that coverage may only be available for certain health care providers and that prior authorization may be required for certain services. Employers may also intervene in certain disputes between the insurer and the employee. Under this system, choices employers make about which plans to offer may result in dissatisfaction among workers who find that certain treatments are no longer covered or that they must change health care providers.

Risks for employees

As the cost and risks to employers has increased, so too have the risks to employees.

Financial risks. As noted earlier, employees are expected to bear a greater portion of health care costs now than in the past. As a result, more employees are declining to enroll in health insurance plans even when employers offer the plans. Between 1989 and 1996, 76.4 percent of the decline in employer health coverage was the result of growth in the required employee premium contribution (AFL-CIO 1996). In addition, even employees with health care coverage may face problems obtaining and paying for care.

Coverage risks. In the past decade, choosing a plan has increasingly meant choosing a specific set of physicians, hospitals, laboratories, and a specific drug formulary. Thus, the choices made by employers determine the type of health care employees will receive and who will provide the care. When employers change the coverage they offer, employees may discover that physicians associated with their former plan or services covered by their old plan are no longer covered.

For most working-age people and their dependents, these restrictions may be simply a matter of convenience; but, for a few chronically ill or disabled persons and for some uniquely acute illnesses, these differences may have a direct bearing on the course of their care. A change in plans can be devastating if people are forced to rebuild the network of providers who understand their condition. This may be the largest single risk an individual with a health condition faces—that their particular ailment might be better served under a particular health plan that their employer no longer offers or by a provider whose services are no longer covered by the plan.[2]

Changes in the source of care may interrupt the continuity of health care and have an impact on the quality of care received, but people in approximately 12 percent of American families changed their usual source of health care within a one year period in 1996. Among those people, 25 percent of the families with members who changed their usual source of care made the change for reasons related to their insurance coverage. For example, they changed health insurance plans or they were forced to change doctors because the insurance plan changed the doctors with whom they contract (U.S. Department of Health and Human Services 1997d, figure 1). In a 1997 national survey of health insurance, one-third of adults aged 18–64 reported that they had been in their current health plan for less than two years (Kaiser Family Foundation and The Commonwealth Fund 1997).

Employees must learn to navigate the system. Each health plan has its own unique set of administrative procedures, and changes in these procedures happen frequently. Employees are expected not only to understand the plan rules when they enroll but also to be aware of and adapt to changes as they occur.

Is the System at Risk?

The pressures to control costs that have been brought about by health care payers, the active interventions of employers, the movement towards managed care, and the tremendous consolidation of resources in those plans could dramatically alter the delivery of health care. There is real potential for the organization of health care services to become more efficient for the patient and actually improve the quality of care for those who need considerable health care services. There is no guarantee that the net result will improve the delivery of care, however. It could just as easily result in greater variation in access to care and even larger variations in the quality of care and not necessarily at a lower relative price. Some of the current influences on the health insurance system are discussed below.

Market segmentation

The system of voluntary, employer-based coverage has certain advantages. The large employer offers a logical grouping of people that facilitates the easy pooling of risk and dissemination of information. An employer-based group offers economies of scale for administration and communication. Large employers are able to negotiate favorable terms and have the market power to smooth disputes between employees and health plans. Some large employers have worked with insurers to develop new health insurance products and some have developed their own insurance plans. Lower administrative and marketing costs and a lower risk premium all combine to make the average cost per insured person in a larger group less than the cost in a smaller group for the same amount of coverage.

The relative success of larger employers has, however, accelerated the natural tendency of the market to segment into smaller risk pools. It is quite natural for health insurers to seek larger groups with smaller proportions of higher risk individuals and avoid smaller groups, particularly those with large proportions of higher risk individuals. Many of the decisions insurers make about prices, benefits, providers, and sales approaches are designed to avoid high-risk groups and to attract lower risk groups. Market segmentation thus increases risks for smaller employers or those with higher cost workers.

The move to managed care

The use of managed care plans has been cited as an effective method for controlling health care costs. There is some question, however, about the level of future savings that can be achieved. Most managed care savings stem from the economies of scale of integrating providers and volume discounts to a large purchaser. Additional savings will require more effective and efficient management of care itself. Far too many health plans, however, have devoted their resources to the integration of providers and attaining market shares. Fewer plans have invested in the management information systems necessary to more effectively manage health care. In addition, premiums could rise if proposals to increase flexibility for consumers in managed care plans are enacted.

Another trend related to managed care is that, in just the last few years, very large, publicly held managed care companies have been purchasing and consolidating providers. This integration could dramatically alter the supply side of the market and could have a real impact on the costs of health care in the future. What is less clear about this movement is how pervasive this trend will be and whether certain populations will have less access to health care because of the changing distribution of providers. It is also less clear whether these organizations will be able to sustain the growth achieved by merging and consolidating.

Political responses

Political responses to an unstable insurance market will also have consequences for the health insurance system. Inadequacies in the employer-provided health insurance market have been the basis for proposals for a national public program that all employers would be required to help finance. This seems less likely in the current political climate than public actions to make incremental changes in the health care system, particularly actions to stabilize the market, subsidize some of the uninsured to help them into the market, and segment the market in a rational way. Most states have undertaken each of these activities, although they have done so differently and with different emphasis. In addition, the federal government has based new federal standards on ongoing activities in states.

In an effort to stabilize the market, for example, most states have worked towards limiting medical underwriting and guaranteeing that anyone willing and able to purchase insurance will be able to do so. More recently, on the federal level, the Health Insurance Portability and Accountability Act of 1996 (HIPAA) supports state efforts and makes changes in the tax code that would subject self-insured plans to many of the same provisions applied to state regulated plans. This act was recently implemented and many of the state insurance reforms are also recent so it is too soon to know how the market will change. It is not likely, however, that the reforms will lower the cost of health insurance. In fact, it is more likely that prices will rise. If health insurance companies are forced to broaden risk pools and take on more risk, they may raise premiums. As a consequence, firms that do not yet offer health insurance but are planning to do so may delay implementing their plans for financial reasons. It is more likely, however, that these firms will have access to health insurance when they decide to make the purchase.

Efforts to provide health insurance to those without coverage have also occurred on the state and federal levels. In the last several years, the number of state-sponsored health insurance programs for the uninsured has increased. Beginning in 1987, Congress passed a series of laws to expand eligibility for pregnant women and children in the Medicaid program and gave states the flexibility to further expand program eligibility. The State Children's Health Insurance Program provides states with funds to provide coverage for low-income uninsured children who do not qualify for Medicaid. States have aggressive outreach campaigns to find and enroll uninsured children. There is some concern that employers may not feel compelled to offer health insurance if publicly subsidized insurance is available. Policymakers note, however, that many low-wage workers are employed at firms that have not offered insurance in the past because it is either unavailable or unaffordable.

OVERVIEW OF THE CANADIAN HEALTH CARE SYSTEM

This section begins with a brief description of the system of health care in Canada. The compelling demographic change and its implications for public finance of pay-as-you-go programs, including health care, are then presented.

Universal Coverage

A fundamental difference between the U.S. and Canadian health care systems is that decisions that Canadian employers make do not have an impact on employee's access to most health care. Access to health care in Canada is universal. For the most part, access to care in Canada is unrelated to employment status or to the type of compensation offered by employers. Therefore, health care coverage is not a factor that people must consider when they think about changing jobs.

The Canadian constitution gives jurisdiction over health care to the provinces and territories. Thus, what is commonly referred to as "Canada's system of public health care" is really 10 provincial and 2 territorial health care systems, bound by a set of common principles enunciated in the Canada Health Act. The five key principles of the system are public administration (nonprofit delivery by public authorities accountable to the provincial government), comprehensiveness (provision of all medically necessary service), universality (coverage of the entire population), accessibility (reasonable access to services without barriers), and portability of health care coverage across jurisdictions.

"Socialized Medicine"?

While Canada's system of health care is often referred to as "socialized medicine," there are at least two aberrations from a pure socialized medicine model. First, most physicians are not employees of the state. Physicians, in private or group practice, bill the provincial health care authority on a fee-for-service basis, although the fees that physicians can charge are negotiated, usually between the provincial government and representatives of physicians. Physicians cannot bill patients directly for services, nor can they ask patients to pay an amount above that paid by the provincial health authority.

Second, a considerable and growing proportion of Canadian health care financing is private, including expenditures by health insurance companies, out-of-pocket expenditures by individuals, and patient services paid by individuals or insurance companies (e.g., for nonmedically essential services, private hospital rooms, etc.). While real public sector health expenditures have been falling since 1994, private expenditures have been growing at 4 percent per year (Table 4.1). Indeed, private health expenditures became an increasingly important component of total public and private health expenditures during the 1990s and grew faster than public sector expenditures in every year since

1991. In 1996, the proportion of public to total financing had fallen to 69.9 percent, while the private sector contribution increased to 30.1 percent, compared with 74.6 percent and 25.4 percent, respectively, in 1991. For additional perspective, the percentages were 76.4 percent public and 23.6 percent private in 1975. It should also be noted that, due to changes in the funding formula, the proportion of provincial health expenditures financed by the federal government fell from 41 percent to 32 percent between 1977 and 1995.

Rising Costs

Total health care costs were slightly over $75 billion in 1996, or 9.5 percent of Gross Domestic Product. While real expenditures have been increasing through the 1990s, the 1996 share was down from a high of 10.2 percent in 1992, but up considerably from 7 percent in the 1970s (Health Canada 1997).

The public health care system is financed through taxation of individuals, businesses, and corporations in addition to borrowing by the federal and provincial governments. In two provinces, Alberta and British Columbia, health care premiums are assessed, but nonpayment of the premium has no impact on eligibility for health services. Both the federal and provincial governments share the costs of financing health care costs, but the cost-sharing formula has evolved over time. Initially, the federal government financed approximately 50 percent of each province's health care expenditures. From 1977 to 1996, the federal government provided transfers to the provinces (which covered federal contributions to both health care and postsecondary education) based on the notion that per capita expenditures on essential government services should be approximately equal and not vary substantially from province to province. Since 1996, the federal contribution has been lump-sum transfers in the form of money and relinquishing "tax room" (i.e., the federal government lowers personal and/or corporate tax rates, allowing the provinces to increase tax rates with no net impact on the tax burden to individuals or corporations).

In common with the United States, Canadian governments have been concerned about the growing costs of health care. Health care costs are the single largest line item of provincial government budgets and, as such, have been a source of careful scrutiny by politicians seek-

Table 4.1 Public and Private Health Expenditures in Canada, 1990–1996[a]

Category	1990	1991	1992	1993	1994	1995	1996
Total ($, billions)	61.2	66.4	70.1	71.8	73.0	74.3	75.2
Real change (%)	2.97	3.84	2.47	1.08	0.71	0.66	0.56
Per capita ($)	2,201	2,362	2,456	2,480	2,496	2,509	2,511
Public sector ($, billions)	45.6	49.6	52.0	52.5	52.6	52.8	52.6
Real change (%)	2.85	4.06	1.99	0.26	–0.38	–0.57	–0.74
Per capita	1,643	1,763	1,820	1,812	1,800	1,783	1,754
Private sector ($, billions)	15.5	16.8	18.2	19.3	20.4	21.5	22.7
Real change (%)	3.35	3.17	3.96	3.58	3.95	4.16	4.08
Per capita ($)	558	599	636	668	696	726	757

SOURCE: Health Canada (1997).

[a] Total, public sector, private sector, and all per capita expenditures are in current Canadian dollars.

ing to control and eliminate budget deficits. In addition, Canada's demographic structure is changing in ways that put at risk the sustainability of all manner of pay-as-you-go financed programs, especially those geared toward the elderly population.

Fiscal pressures have caused all levels of government to reevaluate their expenditures. Since health expenditures account for about one-third of total provincial expenditures, they are an obvious target for retrenchment. Combined with substantial reductions in federal transfers to the provinces, the health care system has come under considerable restraint in virtually all jurisdictions in Canada. The recent decline in public health expenditures and the growing proportion of health care financing from private sources reflect public sector retrenchment in health services financing in Canada. Recent efforts to restructure the delivery of services have been aimed at containing public health care costs, although it is a source of considerable debate as to whether these reforms are harming or improving health services for Canadians.

Demographic Changes and Their Implications
for Pay-As-You-Go Financing

Canada's system of health care is financed on a pay-as-you-go basis. That is, health expenses are financed in the year in which they are incurred. The federal government and most provincial governments have experienced extended periods of budget deficits resulting in considerable accumulation of public debt, relative to the size of the economy. Finding ways to respond to budget deficits, public debt, and debt-servicing costs has become a preoccupation for governments. Concurrent with the period of public debt accumulation, the demographic profile of Canada has been evolving. In response, policymakers have begun to evaluate the costs of public programs on broader terms than annual changes in the budget balance, considering also their intergenerational implications (Auditor General of Canada 1998).

This new intergenerational perspective creates challenges because it opens a debate that Canadians have been largely able to avoid. Passing the costs of current programs on to future generations of Canadians has been expedient, largely because the generations to whom the costs were passed were not yet born, and therefore not heard, when these funding decisions were made. As Canada's demographic structure has changed, so has the need to carefully consider expanded funding of pay-as-you-go programs and to make difficult reforms to ensure the economic sustainability and political viability of cherished programs like public health care.

Pay-as-you-go financing of programs can be a reasonable approach to providing generous benefits when the size of the working age population, relative to the size of the population receiving benefits is large and stable over time. Until recently, this had been the situation in Canada. However, this situation is changing dramatically for three fundamental reasons: 1) an aging population, 2) a continuing increase in life expectancies, and 3) a decline in fertility.

The combination of these factors with the reliance on pay-as-you-go financing has led to concern about the long-run viability of Canada's health care system. Public policy concern with the issue of intergenerational equity is heightened by the fact that the aging of the Canadian population not only places upward pressure on the cost of

Canada's health care programs, but also on the cost of Canada's public pension programs, which are also financed on a pay-as-you-go basis.

The aging of the population will also affect system costs. Older Canadians are the largest per capita consumers of publicly financed health care services. Per capita spending on health care increases substantially with age. For perspective, in 1994, public health expenditures averaged $7,040 for Canadians age 65 and older. In contrast, per capita public sector health expenditures were $647 for those aged 0–14, $846 for those aged 15–44, and $1,563 for those aged 45–64.

It should be noted that health care is only one of a number of larger public programs financed on a pay-as-you-go basis. For example, federal government income support for elderly Canadians is provided through three programs: Old Age Security (OAS), the Guaranteed Income Supplement (GIS), and the Canada Pension Plan (CPP). The Canada Pension Plan provides a timely example of the pressures facing pay-as-you-go government programs from which net benefits (benefits received less contributions) are heavily weighted toward the elderly population and the policy responses to these pressures.

Like the Social Security system in the United States, CPP has undergone a number of reforms. Among these was a sharp rise in the actual contribution rate, from the current level of 5.85 percent to 9.9 percent in 2003. The latter is estimated to be the "steady-state" rate—that is, the contribution rate necessary to fully fund new benefits and to service the existing unfunded liability. The purpose of the sharp and rapid increase in contribution rates was twofold: 1) to forestall the larger increase in contribution rates that would otherwise be required and 2) to increase the degree of funding, thereby lessening the extent to which the CPP is financed on a pay-as-you-go basis. In the absence of this reform, the (pay-as-you-go) contribution rate would have risen from the current pay-as-you-go contribution rate of 8.00 percent in 1997 to 14.22 percent in 2030, an increase of 77.8 percent. As emphasized earlier, the purpose of these reforms was to promote intergenerational equity by reducing (but not eliminating) the extent to which younger workers will pay higher contributions for the same (or lower) level of benefits.

There are no official projections of the pay-as-you-go tax rates necessary to finance Canada's health care system. However, the Auditor General of Canada has released projections of the ratio of government spending on Canada's public pension programs (CPP/QPP, OAS [including SPA and WSPA], GIS) and on health care to gross domestic product (GDP) from the present to the year 2031 (Auditor General of Canada1998). These figures demonstrate the projected costs of these programs as a proportion of the entire economy, not just employment earnings. These projections show that demographically driven increases in public spending on pensions and on health care represent a major challenge to fiscal planning in the years ahead. Under the median scenario for health care costs, government spending on these items will rise from 11.6 percent of GDP in 1996 to 17.2 percent (a 48 percent increase) by 2031. Health care costs are, by far, the largest single component of these costs and are projected to rise from 6.4 percent of GDP to 9.0 percent.

POLICY OPTIONS FOR THE UNITED STATES AND CANADA

Few Canadians would see the U.S. health care system as ideal, and few Americans think the Canadian system is flawless. Yet, policy options under consideration in each country could make the systems far more alike than they have been in the past.

United States

The Canadian system has universal coverage and is plagued by costs. In contrast, coverage is the U.S. system's most important problem, although costs are certainly a close second.

Most U.S. policymakers have abandoned, at least for now, the goal of achieving universal coverage by means of a single, sweeping reform. The wave of the future seems to be specialized remedies such as those already passed on behalf of people leaving or changing jobs or abandoning welfare for the work place, but the incremental road to universal health care coverage (most people's ultimate goal) may not be direct. Most of the easy coverage fixes—and probably some that are not so easy—have been enacted. Yet, growing numbers of Ameri-

cans—many of them full-time, full-year workers or their families—
remain without coverage or the near-term prospect of obtaining it.

Those with coverage, in turn, can expect incremental efforts to
improve their negotiating power against insurance companies and
health care plans that take a narrow view (at least in the patient's eyes)
of what constitutes medically necessary health care. While "patient
rights" is the new watchword for health system reformers, "patient
responsibility" is the unspoken but necessary corollary. Patients have
more medical choices than ever before, but plans have more reasons
and ways to limit them. Only the determined and informed patient will
be able to protect and exercise all rights the states or the federal government may declare.

Canada

Some years ago, Mike Myers, a Canada-born comedian, said the
Canadian health insurance system is one of the top five things Canadians like best about their country (another of the five was Florida).
While Canadians probably still like Florida, it would be interesting to
know whether the health care coverage system would make the top-five
list today. Fiscal pressures have led to major changes in the system,
including reductions in inpatient care, expanded community services,
and consolidation of hospitals under regional authorities (Naylor
1999). These changes have shaken public confidence in the system.
Ongoing challenges include integrating services across the continuum
of care, standardizing prescription drug coverage, reforming physician
payment practices, and measuring and managing the quality of care.
This incremental agenda is seen as the best way for Canada to sustain
and improve its single-payer system.

What are the real and perceived implications of government
restraint in health care expenditures for Canadian workers? First, if it
is true that reduced government expenditures are truly harmful, then an
obvious implication could be compromised health. There is considerable debate about whether recent reductions in health expenditures
have been harmful (see, for example, Drache and Sullivan 1999; Evans
1999). The Canadian health care system has been heavily reliant on
the hospital as the key center for providing health care. Recent reforms
have focused on restructuring health care, such that less is provided in

hospitals, the most costly mode, and more through community and home-based services. Nonetheless, a reduction in hospital resources can lead to a general perception that the public health care system is failing and that more drastic alternatives need be found.

Pressure to contain direct government expenditures may lead to the introduction of user fees for some services, the de-listing (or non-listing) of services that are "medically necessary" and therefore financed by provincial health authorities, or the "under-provision" of services resulting in queues for even some medically necessary services. To varying degrees, all of these have begun to appear in Canada.

Taken together, a loss of confidence in the public health care system, real or perceived, could result in the deeper participation of private care providers and insurers into the Canadian health care system. There is clearly an open debate about the extent to which private versus public provision of health care services, or some combination, is optimal. This debate is clearly beyond the purview of this chapter. However, there is no evidence that private provision of health care results in better health outcomes, or superior cost containment, relative to public provision. Further movement of the Canadian system in this direction could be expected to introduce the same types of issues discussed in the U.S. context previously in this chapter.

CONCLUSIONS

Canadian and U.S. workers face health care risks very differently. Most Americans under age 65 depend on their employers for health care coverage. Employers, in turn, are shifting more of the cost and risk of health care coverage to their employees. To the extent that policymakers address these risks, it will probably be to shift more of these risks back to employers and health care plans.

For Canadians, health care risks are pooled in the political marketplace, not the labor market. But, to the extent that Canadians see themselves as being harmed by the ongoing restructuring of their health care system, they are bound to consider other approaches to delivering health care, including a greater role for private provision. Given the

U.S. experience, it is an open question whether this will result in Canadian workers leaping from the frying pan into the fire.

Notes

1. Beginning in 1987, Congress passed a series of laws to expand eligibility for pregnant women and children in the Medicaid program and gave states the flexibility to further expand program eligibility. The recently established State Children's Health Insurance Program provides states with funds to provide coverage for low-income uninsured children who do not qualify for Medicaid.
2. Until recently, employers were also at risk if they had to sign with a new insurer and there was a requirement for a waiting period before treatment for pre-existing conditions would be covered. With the passage of the Health Insurance Portability and Accountability Act (HIPAA) of 1996, the risk to employees has substantially been reduced. HIPAA does protect employees when they change to new health plans by transferring existing credit under the old plan to the new plan. Furthermore, the waiting period before treatment for preexisting conditions would be covered has been limited to 12 months. Nevertheless, the exceptions involved that still make it difficult for employers to completely transfer their credit to the new plan.

References

AFL-CIO. 1996. *Paying More and Losing Ground—How Employer Cost-Shifting is Eroding Health Coverage of Working Families.* Washington, D.C.: American Federation of Labor and Congress of Industrial Organizations.

Auditor General of Canada. 1998. *Report of the Auditor General of Canada to the House of Commons. Ottawa,* April.

Bennefield, Robert L. 1997. "Health Insurance Coverage: 1996." *Current Population Reports*, U.S. Census Bureau, September, pp. 60–199.

Drache, Daniel, and Terry Sullivan, eds. 1999. *Health Reform: Public Success, Private Failure.* New York: Routledge.

Employee Benefit Research Institute. 1997a. *Trends in Health Insurance Coverage.* Issue Brief Number 185, Washington, D.C., May.

_____. 1997b. *Trends in Health Insurance Coverage*, Issue Brief Number 191, Washington, D.C., November.

_____. 1997c. "Health Coverage among Part-Timers." *EBRI Notes* 18(9).

_____. 1997d. *EBRI Databook on Employee Benefits.* Fourth ed., Washington, D.C.: Employee Benefit Research Institute

Evans, Robert. 1999. "Health Reform: What 'Business' is it of Business?" In *Health Reform: Public Success, Private Failure,* Daniel Drache and Terry

Sullivan, eds., New York: Routledge, pp. 25–47.

Executive Office of the President. 1999. *Economic Report of the President 1999*. Washington, D.C.: U.S. Government Printing Office.

Ginsburg, Paul B., Jon R. Gabel, and Kelly A. Hunt. 1998. "Tracking Small-Firm Coverage, 1989–1996." *Health Affairs* 17(1): 167–171.

Health Canada. 1997. "National Health Expenditures in Canada, 1975–1996 Fact Sheets." Policy and Consultation Branch, Ottawa.

Kaiser Family Foundation and The Commonwealth Fund. 1997. *Working Families at Risk: Coverage, Access, Costs and Worries*. Kaiser/Commonwealth 1997 National Survey of Health Insurance, December.

KPMG Peat Marwick LLP. 1997. *Health Benefits in 1997*. Washington, D.C.: KPMG, June.

Levit, Katharine R., Helen C. Lazenby, Bradley R. Braden, and the National Accounts Team. 1998. "National Health Spending Trends in 1996." *Health Affairs* 17(1): 35–51.

Liska, David, et al. 1997. *Medicaid Expenditures and Beneficiaries, National State Profiles and Trends, 1990–1995*. Washington, D.C., Kaiser Commission on the Future of Medicaid.

Naylor, David C. 1999. "Health Care in Canada: Incrementalism under Fiscal Duress." *Health Affairs* 18(May/June): 9–26.

Price Waterhouse LLP. 1995. "Do Medicare HMOs Reduce Fees for Service Costs?" Press release, September 13.

Rowland, Diane. 1995. "Medicaid: The Health and Long-Term Safety Net." Testimony before the Committee on Finance, United States Senate, June 29.

Schoen, Cathy, Barbara Lyons, Diane Rowland, Karen Davis, and Elaine Puleo. 1997. "Insurance Matters for Low-Income Adults: Results from a Five-State Survey." *Health Affairs* 16(5): 163–171.

Silow-Carroll, Andrew, Jack A. Meyer, Marsha Regenstein, and Nancy Bagby. 1995. *In Sickness and in Health? The Marriage between Employers and Health Care*. Washington, D.C.: The Economic and Social Research Institute.

U.S. Bureau of the Census. 1997a. *Statistical Abstract of the United States 1997*. Washington, D.C.: U.S. Government Printing Office.

_____. 1997b. *Current Population Reports*. U.S. Census Bureau, March.

U.S. Department of Health and Human Services. 1997a. *Health Care Financing Review, Medicare and Medicaid Statistical Supplement, 1997*.

_____. 1997b. *Health Insurance Status of the Civilian Noninstitutionalized Population: 1996*. Research Findings #1, Publication 97-0030, August.

_____. 1997c. *Health Insurance Status of the Workers and Their Families: 1996*. Research Findings #2, Publication 97-0065, September.

_____. 1997d. *Access to Health Care—Sources and Barriers: 1996*. Research Findings #3, Publication 98-0001, October.

5

Risk Sharing through Social Security Retirement Income Systems

John A. Turner

Risk bearing by workers is reduced by risk sharing through social security. The social security programs in Canada and the United States provide social insurance that reduces risk bearing by workers and their families. Perhaps because of societal differences between the two countries concerning views as to the role of government, the Canadian and U.S. programs differ in ways that affect the amount of risk workers bear.

Being tied to employment, social security contributions by employers for employees are part of employee compensation. The employer and employee share of contributions together equal 6 percent of covered wages in Canada, where social security is partially financed by general revenue. In the United States, which relies primarily on payroll tax financing, equal contributions by employers and employees total 12.4 percent of covered wages.

The compensation value to workers of social security and occupational pension plans is measured not by contributions, however, because they may bear little relationship to ultimate benefits. Rather, the value is measured by the increase in the actuarial present value of future benefits that occurs due to having worked. This value historically has been far greater than the value of contributions, but the difference has diminished considerably over time and has reversed for some high-wage workers in the United States.

While most analyses of retirement benefits focus on the expected level of pension benefits, the riskiness of retirement benefits and their risk-bearing aspects are also important to workers. A simple measure of the riskiness of retirement benefits is the variability in their real value. The riskiness is affected by factors affecting the accrual of real pension benefits up to retirement and by factors affecting the variability in the real value of benefits once benefit payments have started.

Retirement benefits are subject to a number of risks affecting the probability of receipt and the level of benefits. For example, workers in a job covered by social security or an occupational pension do not necessarily receive a pension when they retire. In social security and in occupational plans, retirees will not receive benefits if they have not worked long enough to qualify.

Ultimately, the simple measure of the riskiness of retirement benefits is inadequate because the riskiness of retirement benefits cannot be determined in isolation. Financial theory indicates that risk can be considered only in the context of the total portfolio held by the retiree or worker. The correlation of pension risk with other risks the worker faces should be considered. To the extent that retirement benefit risks are positively correlated with job risks, the effects of the retirement benefit risks are more serious. To the extent that retirement benefit risks offset job-related risks, the variability in retirement benefits plays an insurance role.

The primary income-producing asset of most workers is their job, which often has risks that are positively correlated with the risks of an occupational pension plan, if one is provided. For example, traditional pension plans tend to reward longevity on a job and thus any factor that increases the risk of losing one's job also adversely affects the value of the pension. Social security, however, is an important part of the wealth portfolio of most workers and is structured so as to offset job-related risks, for example, by allowing workers to exclude periods of low earnings when calculating benefit levels.

RISK BEARING IN RETIREMENT INCOME SYSTEMS

Retirement pension plans are either defined benefit or defined contribution. A defined benefit plan determines the benefit payable by applying a formula to the worker's years of service and earnings. Frequently, the benefit is based on an average of the worker's highest three or five years of earnings. A defined contribution plan, by contrast, is like a mutual fund account. The account balance is determined by employer and employee contributions and the investment earnings on those contributions. The social security systems in both Canada and the United States use a pay-as-you-go or partially funded defined benefit plan for the majority of benefits, tying benefits to wage-indexed average wages over the worker's lifetime.

In structuring social security systems, a trade-off occurs between providing incentives and providing risk bearing. When perfectly tied to wages, social security benefits can be considered to be a wage supplement, but no risk bearing by social security is provided because the variability in workers' compensation is unchanged. Risk bearing by social security can be provided by making the benefit formula progressive, with higher wage workers receiving less generous benefits relative to their wages. Income redistribution can be considered an aspect of risk bearing concerning income-related risks.

Workers face a number of different risks, including wage risk and longevity risk, that social security may alleviate. The remainder of this section considers effects of social security on various types of risk bearing by workers.

Wage Risk

Workers face risks in the level of their wages over their life cycles. Unanticipated changes in labor market conditions they face cause risk to wage income. This risk occurs both through variation in wage rates and work hours.

Early Retirement Risk

As a result of risks in the later part of working life, including unemployment and poor health, social security early retirement benefits have been offered.

For workers with a life expectancy shorter than the actuarial life expectancy, early retirement benefits provided with an actuarial reduction for taking them early are more generous in terms of lifetime present value than are normal retirement benefits available at a later age. This feature of defined benefit social security insures an initial benefit level to employees who are unable to work past early retirement.

Longevity Risk

Workers who do not annuitize their assets risk outliving their assets. Social security programs in both Canada and the United States insure against this risk by providing annuities rather than lump sum benefits.

Demographic Risk

Pay-as-you-go social security plans face demographic risk due to an increasing old-age dependency ratio raising the cost of providing retirement benefits. However, changes in the percentage of the elderly population can be predicted fairly accurately years in advance, and thus could be considered cost factors rather than risk factors. Only unexpected changes would be risk factors.

Inflation Risk

Inflation risk affects the initial real value of benefits and the value of benefits in payment to retirees. Both the Canadian and U.S. social security systems protect against inflation risk during retirement by providing cost-of-living adjustments.

Political Risk

Workers face political risk with respect to their retirement benefits because the government can change the value of their benefits at any time. While social security systems are evolving institutions in both Canada and the United States, the political risk is relatively small because of the stability of the governmental systems and the ability of the social security systems to foresee potential future problems and propose solutions far in advance.

SOCIAL SECURITY IN CANADA

The social security programs in Canada are relatively young. Because provision of old-age benefits was not considered to fall under the constitutional authority granted the Canadian government, the Canadian Constitution was amended in 1951 to allow the government to provide pensions for the elderly under the Old Age Security Act. It was amended again in 1964 to authorize the inclusion of survivor and disability benefits in the Canada Pension Plan (CPP), which became effective on January 1, 1966. At that time, the province of Quebec exercised its constitutional right to opt out of the national plan and set up the Quebec Pension Plan (QPP). The Quebec plan is similar to the CPP, which applies in the other nine provinces. There is full portability between the CPP and the QPP.

Canada provides public pensions through a combination of three national programs: the Old Age Security (OAS), the Guaranteed Income Supplement (GIS), Spouse's Allowance, and the Canada or Quebec Pension Plans. The OAS pension provides a universal demogrant (flat benefit) to all persons aged 65 and over who have lived in Canada at least 10 years, with benefits increasing for up to 40 years of residence after age 18. The benefit is financed from general revenues and equals approximately 15 percent of the lifetime average (wage-indexed) wage of the average worker, with a higher percentage for lower income workers. These benefits increase quarterly during retirement for changes in the cost of living.

The GIS and Spouse's Allowance programs provide benefits subject to an income test, also for people aged 65 and older who are recipients of an OAS pension. The monthly benefit depends on marital status and income. Even though it is income tested, the GIS is not a poverty program like the Supplemental Security Income program in the United States. Approximately 40 percent of the elderly who receive an OAS benefit also receive a GIS benefit (Tamagno 1996). Above a certain income level, the GIS benefit is reduced $1 for every $2 in income.

The Spouse's Allowance may be paid to the spouse of an OAS pensioner, or to a widow or widower, who is between the ages of 60 and 64 and who has lived in Canada for at least 10 years after age 18. The Spouse's Allowance stops when the person becomes eligible for an OAS pension at age 65. The GIS and Spouse's Allowance are financed out of general revenue.

The U.S. retirement income system is generally characterized as having three tiers—social security, private pensions, and private savings. If the Canadian retirement income system is analyzed in the same way, it can be thought of as having four tiers. The OAS and the GIS together form one tier that does not have a direct counterpart in the United States. These programs are distinct from U.S. social security benefits as a source of retirement income and as a retirement income tier in that neither benefits are tied to the number of years worked or to previous contributions.

The CPP and QPP provide earnings-related benefits for those who contributed during their working lives and represent the second tier of the Canadian retirement income system. They are a less important source of benefits than are social security benefits in the United States because they are supplemented by OAS and GIS benefits. The benefits from the C/QPP are linked to the individual's average lifetime covered earnings, and the payroll tax supporting these programs only applies to income up to the national average wage, which was Can.\$37,400 in 1999.

This low ceiling on taxable income limits the amount of redistribution that can occur through this program because it limits the social security contribution liability of upper income workers. An explanation for the relatively low ceiling on social security taxable earnings relates to the fact that social security was developed relatively late in Canada. At the time it was developed, many high-income workers had occupational pension plans, and Canadian policymakers did not want the social security system to displace those plans.

The CPP replaces 25 percent of the worker's average lifetime earnings for persons whose earnings are less than or equal to the average industrial wage, compared with 40 percent for social security in the United States. For higher earners, the replacement rate is progressively lower in both countries.

The Canadian programs provide a survivor benefit to surviving spouses but do not provide a spouse benefit while both husband and wife are alive. The OAS benefit, which is provided to all retirees individually rather than on a family basis, corresponds in function to the spouse benefit in the U.S. social security system. Participation in the C/QPP is compulsory for all workers with earned income between the ages of 18 and 70, whether employed or self-employed, including government workers. This pension may be taken as early as age 60 in reduced amount or may be deferred until age 70 with an increased benefit to compensate for postponed receipt.

Income below a low level is exempted from the social security payroll tax for all workers. The exemption does not affect the earnings level used to calculate benefits. The exemption thus adds an element of progressivity not present in the U.S. system because it reduces the average tax rate for low wage workers more than it does for high-wage workers.

When the CPP "matures," or has existed long enough to cover a worker's entire career from age 18 to age 65, Canadians will be allowed to drop 7 of their nonworking or low income years between ages 18 and 65 (or 15 percent of the years between age 18 and the age at which CPP benefits are first received, if younger than 65) when calculating benefits. Up to that point, workers can drop 15 percent of their working years after 1965 or after age 18, whichever occurred later. This feature provides insurance against periods of unemployment or downward wage fluctuations for low-wage workers who start working at age 18. The drop-out years for workers with graduate education who start working at age 25 are entirely taken by their education, leaving them no drop out years during their working career. Unemployment is less likely to occur for those workers, however.

Contributors can also exclude time out of the workforce caring for children under age seven, with no limit on the number of years excluded. These drop-out years particularly help women because regulations make it difficult for men to qualify.

The third tier of the Canadian retirement income system is formed by the occupational pension system and the individual, voluntary, tax-assisted plans known as Registered Retirement Savings Plans (RRSPs) (which are similar to Individual Retirement Accounts in the United States. The fourth tier is personal savings. In both countries, the labor market earnings of households with retirement age workers could be thought of as an additional tier.

Table 5.1 shows the relative importance of Canadian social security benefits at different levels of worker income. The total public pension upon retirement at age 65 for a single person is roughly 46 percent of earnings at the average level of earnings for a full career worker, more for lower income workers and less for higher income workers. Because the OAS benefits, GIS, and Spouse's Allowances are not

Table 5.1 Retirement Income from Government Programs, 1993 (Can.$)[a]

Employment income prior to retirement (Can.$)	OAS	GIS	C/QPP	Total	Employment income (%)
0	4,547	5,404		9,951	
5,000	4,547	4,779	1,250	10,576	212
10,000	4,547	4,154	2,500	11,201	112
15,000	4,547	3,529	3,750	11,826	79
20,000	4,547	2,904	5,000	12,451	62
25,000	4,547	2,279	6,250	13,076	52
30,000	4,547	1,654	7,500	13,701	46

SOURCE: Maser (1995).

[a] Prior to age 65, persons with very low employment income could also receive social assistance benefits. This would lower the total income replacement rate. This table shows approximate annual amounts based on rates in January 1993 that a 65-year-old single person could expect to receive from these public programs. These amounts assume the individual has no other income, meets the residency requirements for full OAS benefits, and has contributed the required time to the C/QPP.

related to preretirement earnings, they are relatively more important for low-income workers. Public pension benefits are fairly flat, increasing little with preretirement income, because OAS benefits do not increase with income, and CPP benefits are modest, capped, and effectively subject to the GIS tax-back (Gunderson, Hyatt, and Pesando 1996). Canada ties retirement benefits less to the preretirement earnings of workers than does the United States.

A special tax, introduced in 1989, applies on OAS and Family Allowance benefits for individuals above a threshold income (approximately Can.$52,000 in 1996, indexed). This tax, derogatorily called a "clawback," is levied at a 15 percent rate on income up to the income level that results in complete elimination of the benefit. The clawback does not apply to C/QPP benefits because these have presumably been paid for by contributions of individuals and their employers. The clawback only affects the top 5 percent of retirees by income (Tamagno 1996).

SOCIAL SECURITY IN THE UNITED STATES

Social security in the United States is financed by a payroll tax levied equally on employers and employees up to a ceiling on earnings that currently covers all earnings of most workers. In 1999, the Old-Age, Survivors and Disability Insurance (OASDI) tax rate was 6.2 percent each for employer and employee on annual earnings up to U.S.$72,600, with no exemption amount, versus 2.8 percent each for Canada Pension Plan contributions on earnings up to Can.$37,400 (U.S.$24,290). Thus, higher income workers pay considerably more through the social security tax in the United States than they do in Canada, both because of a higher tax rate and because more of their earnings are subject to the tax. This difference is offset to some extent by the progressivity of the Canadian income tax system and the use of general revenue financing for an important part of Canadian social security benefits—the first-tier benefits.

Benefits in the United States are based on wage-indexed average earnings over the highest 35 years of earnings. Early retirement old-age benefits (at a reduced rate) are available at age 62, compared with 60 in Canada. Benefits are progressive, being higher relative to preretirement earnings for low-income beneficiaries. Benefits after retirement are price indexed, and an earnings test applies up to age 65 to receive benefits. Spouse benefits equal to 50 percent of the retired worker's benefit are provided to spouses who have never worked or whose earnings provide a benefit less than that received as a spouse benefit. This benefit is available at 65 and is reduced for earlier receipt, with the earliest age being 60.

The United States does not have a separate universal demogrant, like the OAS, that is unrelated to work. It does, however, have a minimum benefit for long-term workers. It also does not have an income-tested supplement like the GIS, but it does have a narrower income-tested benefits program through the anti-poverty Supplemental Security Income (SSI) program.

While differing in important ways, the United States and Canada have basically similar retirement income systems. Rather than having a generous public plan that provides retirees most of their retirement income, as do countries in southern Europe, both have diversified retirement income systems with modest social security benefits that leave room for occupational pensions for higher income workers. Both the Canadian and U.S. social security systems provide a low replacement rate (the ratio of the retiree's benefits to his or her previous earnings) compared with most other OECD countries.

COMPARISON OF RISK SHARING IN THE CANADIAN AND U.S. SOCIAL SECURITY SYSTEMS

Risk sharing in the Canadian and U.S. social security systems can be compared along various aspects of retirement income risk.

Income Replacement

One aspect of retirement income risk is income replacement risk. The social security systems in the two countries can be compared in terms of the income replacement rates they provide. Table 5.2 shows calculated replacement rates provided by social security to workers at different levels of preretirement earnings in both countries. Compared with the United States, social security benefits in Canada are more progressive, being more generous for low-income workers and less generous for high-income workers.

Gunderson, Hyatt, and Pesando (1996) have compared the relative importance within total retirement income of different sources of retirement income in Canada and the United States. The social security component of total retirement income is roughly the same in the two countries, as are the income replacement rates provided by social security to median income workers.

Early Retirement Risk

Workers risk being forced to retire earlier than they had planned. Forced early retirement might arise due to layoffs or poor health. Social security protects against this risk by providing early retirement benefits. The U.S. social security system allows workers to retire at age 62, but benefits are reduced roughly 20 percent from those receivable at age 65. For workers with a life expectancy equal to the popula-

**Table 5.2 Income Replaced by Social Security in the United States
and Canada**

Individual's earnings preretirement (U.S.$)	U.S. replacement rate (%)	Canadian replacement rate (%)
6,450	79	130
12,900	57	71
19,350	50	51
25,800	46	42
51,600	27	21
129,000	11	8

SOURCE: Gunderson, Hyatt, and Pesando (1996).

tion average, this is an actuarially fair reduction in benefits. Workers whose early retirement is due to health factors that cause them to have a shortened life expectancy gain lifetime benefits by having the early retirement option, because, for them, the lifetime value of benefits received at age 62 exceeds that of benefits received starting at age 65.

The Canadian social security system provides better early retirement insurance than does the U.S. system. In Canada, benefits are reduced slightly less at age 62 (18 percent) than in the United States (20 percent). Also, the minimum age at which benefits could be received from the CPP was reduced from 65 to 60 in 1987, so that early retirement benefits can be received two years earlier in Canada than in the United States. If workers could freely borrow against their future social security benefits, or consume other forms of wealth before the minimum age for social security receipt, the age at which those benefits could be received would not matter. Because most workers have little financial assets at retirement, many are liquidity constrained and the earliest age at which social security benefits can be received does affect their consumption and their age at retirement.

Insurance Against Low Earnings Years

Workers face the risk that they will have years of low earnings that will reduce their retirement benefits. Social security can protect against this risk by calculating benefits in a way so that a few years of low earnings will have little negative effect on retirement benefits. Both the Canadian and U.S. social security systems allow workers to exclude some low earnings years from consideration in determining benefits. For workers who suffer a loss in earnings during a period, this provision protects their social security benefits from being reduced by that loss. In the United States, social security benefits for retired workers are based on the highest 35 years of earnings. Workers with more than 35 years of earnings may exclude their lowest years. Thus, someone starting work at age 18 and working to 62 would have 44 years of work and 9 drop-out years. Someone starting at age 22 would have 40 years of work and 5 drop-out years.

In Canada, full career workers eventually will be able to exclude their 7 lowest years of earnings (or 15 percent of their working years, whichever is lower), counting all years from age 18 to age 65. Thus, for current lower income workers who start working at age 18 and retire at age 62, the Canadian system provides fewer drop-out years (6.6 vs. 9), providing less protection against periods of low earnings. For someone starting work at age 22, the pattern is reversed (6 vs. 5).

Progressivity

Progressivity in the social security program provides an element of insurance in that it insures against low income. In a progressive social security system, workers with low income pay lower taxes relative to their income and/or receive higher benefits after tax relative to their income than do workers with higher income.

Progressivity in taxes

In both Canada and the United States, there is a maximum on taxable earnings. Workers earning above the maximum in a year pay no social security taxes on earnings above the maximum. However, earnings above the maximum also do not count in computing social security benefits. In Canada, the maximum level of earnings is much lower than in the United States. This by itself would make the system less progressive in terms of tax payments. However, the exclusion of the first Can.$3,500 of earnings from social security taxes is a progressive feature of the tax support for social security in Canada.

Also, in Canada roughly one-third of the old-age benefits are supported through general revenues. General revenues are a more progressive source of taxes than are social security taxes because of the higher tax rates that apply to higher earners. Thus, overall, it appears that the Canadian system is more progressive in its tax structure supporting social security financing.

Progressivity in benefits

Workers in Canada are eligible to receive social security benefits if they have made one year of contributions. The requirement in the United States is a minimum of 10 years of contributions. Thus, the Canadian system is much more favorable to low tenure workers. In Canada, the first-tier benefits are also a progressive feature because they are unrelated to earnings.

In the United States, the social security benefit formula is progressive. To calculate benefits, the worker's average wage is first calculated, indexing for the growth in average wages. Then, a formula is applied that yields a higher replacement rate for lower average wages. This formula yields a progressive benefit structure when viewing benefits on an annual basis.

The progressivity is offset to some extent by differences in life expectancy associated with lifetime income. Lower income workers tend to have lower life expectancy and thus to receive benefits for fewer years. However, they are also more likely to receive disability and survivor benefits. The net effect of their lower life expectancy on benefit progressivity is an unresolved empirical question.

In Canada, benefits are also related to average wages indexed for the growth in wages. However, the benefits are a flat percentage of average wages varying with years worked but not income, with no progressivity in the earnings-related benefit. Overall, as indicated in Table 5.2, benefits are more progressive in Canada than in the United States.

Taxation of benefits

In both Canada and the United States, benefits of higher income beneficiaries are taxed under the personal income tax, providing an additional element of progressivity in the social security systems. In the United States, the taxation of social security benefits only applies for higher income households. In Canada, the tax applies to all beneficiaries with taxable income. Through provisions in the Canadian income tax system, however, such as the income-tested tax credit for persons aged 65 and over, low-income pensioners do not pay tax on their benefits. In Canada, there is also the "clawback" tax of benefits, which is a surtax on OAS benefits that currently only affects the highest income retirees.

Indexation of Benefits

Indexation of benefits provides insurance against inflation during retirement. Both Canada and the United States provide full annual price indexation of benefits starting at retirement. Canada provides quarterly indexation of benefits for OAS benefits. When inflation is low, the difference between quarterly and annual indexation is unimportant, but Canada provides better protection against inflation in periods of high inflation than does the United States.

Survivor's Benefits

In Canada, a surviving spouse can receive a disability or retirement benefit in addition to an age-dependent survivor's benefit. For a surviving spouse age 65 or older, the survivor's benefit equals 60 percent of the CPP benefit of the deceased. However, an individual receiving combined benefits can receive no more than the maximum retirement benefit.

Survivor's benefits are more generous in Canada than in the United States for women who have worked, but less generous for women who never worked outside the home. In Canada, a surviving wife who had never worked outside the home would continue to receive her OAS benefit while that of her husband ends at his death. Thus, she would receive 50 percent of the OAS benefits they both received while her husband was alive. In addition, she would receive 60 percent of the CPP benefit of her husband. She would thus receive between 50 and 60 percent of the benefit received by her and her husband while he was alive. The exact percentage depends on the level of his CPP benefit. A U.S. woman who had never worked would receive 67 percent of the joint benefit received by herself and her husband while he was alive.

A Canadian wife with earnings exactly equal that of her spouse would continue to receive her own CPP and OAS benefits plus 60 percent of her husband's CPP benefit. The percentage she receives of the benefits they received while both were alive depends on the income level of the family, being higher for lower income levels, but would be somewhat higher than 50 percent of their joint benefit. The comparable U.S. woman would receive 50 percent of the joint benefit received by her and her husband while he was alive.

CONCLUSIONS

Both the Canadian and U.S. social security systems have features that reduce the risk bearing of workers with respect to their future retirement income. While in some ways the U.S. system provides greater protection (e.g., for widows who have not worked outside the home), overall it appears the Canadian system provides greater insurance against income risks through its earlier retirement age and greater progressivity of financing and benefits. It is also more favorable to short tenure workers. For most women it provides more generous survivors protection.

References

Gunderson, Morley, Douglas Hyatt, and James E. Pesando. 1996. "Public Pension Plans in the United States and Canada." Prepared for the W.E. Upjohn Insitute Conference on Employee Benefits, Labor Costs, and Labor Markets in Canada and the United States, November 4–6, 1994.

Maser, Karen. 1995. "Who's Saving for Retirement?" *Perspectives on Labour and Income* 7(Winter): 14–19.

Tamagno, Edward. 1996. *Safeguarding Canada's Pension System.* Ottawa: Human Resources Development Canada (Government of Canada).

6

Risk Bearing in Individual and Occupational Pension Plans

James E. Pesando
John A. Turner

INTRODUCTION

Financial risk is inherent in pension plans. It is inherent in their financing and in the accrual of pension rights by workers. It must be borne, but that can be done in different ways—by workers, the employer, an insurance company, stockholders and bondholders of the company, the government (taxpayers), or by other employers.

The rules governing the conditions of benefit payments and required contributions determine who bears pension risk. Some rules are explicit, determined by law, collective bargaining agreements, or the pension benefit formula. Others are implicit or are decided by employers, for example, the circumstances under which the firm will provide cost-of-living adjustments to retirement benefits or terminate the pension plan.

Pension risks in funded pension plans arise in part due to macro-economic risks: nondiversifiable investment risk in financial markets, variability in defined benefit liabilities caused by changing interest rates, and inflation-caused variability in the real value of imperfectly indexed benefits of retirees and in the real value of nominally fixed benefits of job changers. Pension accrual risks for workers arise due to uncertainty in the supply and demand for their labor as well as an uncertain life expectancy.

Pension funds face risks, including political risks arising due to governmental changes in pension regulations. They also face risks due to financial malfeasance by pension fund managers or due to the possibility that the employer will terminate the pension plan in bankruptcy with the plan being insolvent.

Pensions also insure workers against risks. An annuitized pension insures workers against the risks of being unable to work in old age and of outliving one's resources.

Changes in the occupational pension systems in Canada and the United States towards greater reliance on defined contribution plans appear to have shifted risks from employers to workers. The simplest hypothesis for a shift in risk bearing is that the costs of risk bearing by employers have increased. This chapter compares the Canadian and U.S. employer-provided pension systems. While the focus is on the comparison of the two systems, the chapter begins by describing the Canadian system, which is less well-known. Information about the U.S. system is presented as it compares to the Canadian system.

Background

The level of family income in Canada and the United States is roughly equivalent. While average family income is slightly higher (by 2.2 percent) in the United States, median family income is slightly lower (by 4.4 percent), reflecting the greater income inequality in the United States (Wolfson and Murphy 1994).[1]

The elderly in the United States, however, have considerably higher income than they do in Canada—19 percent higher for couples aged 65–74. The mix of income among the elderly also differs. Social security benefits are higher in Canada—6 percent higher for couples aged 65–74, accounting for 40 percent of the income of that group. In comparison, social security benefits account for 31 percent of income for U.S. couples in the same age group. Income from private sources (earnings from working, pensions, and savings) is higher in the United States (Wolfson and Murphy 1994).[2]

The next sections compare the Canadian and U.S. systems of individual and occupational private pension plans and discuss trends in risk bearing. Social security pensions are discussed in Chapter 5.

INDIVIDUAL AND OCCUPATIONAL PENSION PLANS IN CANADA AND THE UNITED STATES

Canadian Pension Plans

In Canada, favorable tax treatment is provided to three types of pension plans: Registered Pension Plans (RPP), Deferred Profit Sharing Plans (DPSP), and Registered Retirement Savings Plans (RRSP). "Registered" refers to federal registration under the Income Tax Act of a plan by a plan sponsor. The term "registered" is the Canadian equivalent to the U.S. term "qualified," which refers to pension plans that qualify for preferential tax treatment under the U.S. Internal Revenue Code. Registered Pension Plans include plans for both private and public sector employees. They are employer-sponsored plans and include both defined benefit and defined contribution plans. Registered Deferred Profit Sharing plans are little used.

Canadian pensions cover 43.4 percent of all employed (government and private sector) workers (45.3 percent of men and 41.1 percent of women). The pension coverage rate for employed workers in the private sector is 31 percent (39 percent for men and 21 percent for women). The coverage rate in the public sector is nearly 100 percent for both men and women. At the beginning of 1996, 48 percent of the members of occupational pension plans were public sector employees, a percentage that has grown over time.

In recent years, the pension coverage rate has been stable. The percentage of the total workforce (including the unemployed) belonging to an employer-provided pension plan ranged from 35 to 37 percent between 1983 and 1993. However, by 1996, participation in employer-provided pension plans was 3 percent lower than the peak in 1992 (Payne 1997). The drop in RPP participation is entirely due to a decline in the participation of men. Layoffs in manufacturing, transportation, and construction, traditionally high coverage industries, explain part of the drop in male pension coverage. Between 1984 and 1994, the percentage of employed women covered by employer-sponsored pension plans increased from 37 to 42 percent, while the percentage of employed men covered fell from 55 to 47 percent. In contrast, the percentage of workers contributing to individual account plans

(RRSPs) almost doubled, growing from 18 percent in 1983 to 35 percent in 1993 (Statistics Canada 1996).

In each year in the early 1990s, about half of Canadian employed workers contributed to at least one of the two most commonly used types of pension plans. Over the period 1991–1993, about 60 percent of employed workers contributed in at least one of the three years. About 40 percent contributed in all three years (Maser 1995). Contributions to RRSPs are voluntary and workers need not contribute each year. Almost half of the participants from 1991 to 1993 contributed in only one or two of the three years. In contrast, most members belonging to an employer-sponsored RPP participated each year because RPP membership is generally compulsory for workers covered by a plan. While access to RPPs is limited because many employers do not offer them, all workers with employment earnings are eligible to save through an RRSP. Most RPP members have the option of adding to their pension savings with RRSP contributions.

The contribution limit to a RRSP is reduced by the previous year's contribution to a pension plan. This feature penalizes job changers who lose pension coverage. They cannot make a full RRSP contribution for a year because they are limited by their previous year's participation in an RPP.

In Canada, RPPs are commonly integrated with social security (the Quebec/Canada Pension Plan). Integration with Old Age Security (OAS) benefits is not permitted in some provinces. Integration means that the RPP benefits are offset by the worker's social security benefits. Among public sector pension participants, 90 percent are in integrated plans. Nearly 80 percent of private sector defined benefit plan members have integrated benefits. By reducing the occupational pension benefits of lower wage workers, integration offsets the progressivity of social security.

Until recently, Canada had a policy of providing tax relief for pension contributions on income up to 2.5 times the average wage. It has, however, frozen the nominal maximum earnings that can receive tax relief so that it is expected that the maximum earnings receiving tax relief will be approximately two times the average wage by 2006. This change will increase the overall progressivity of the retirement income system by reducing the tax subsidy going to high earners.

Most public sector pension plans for government workers provide generous benefits, based on final average earnings, and require members to contribute towards their benefits. These plans usually grant generous survivor benefits and index for inflation. By contrast, private sector plans usually are less generous.

Canadian Pension Regulation

For constitutional reasons, with the exception of applicable tax provisions, occupational pensions are generally regulated by the provincial governments. This causes regional differences in pension regulation. However, certain occupations fall under federal jurisdiction, including the federal public service, the armed forces, the Royal Canadian Mounted Police, and a number of sectors of national importance (e.g., banks, railways, airlines, and communication companies). Pension plans for employees in these categories are regulated directly by the federal government in Ottawa.

A major factor discouraging establishment of new plans in Canada is the complexity of pension laws. The Pension Benefits Acts are detailed and differ among the 11 government authorities (10 provinces plus federal). Laws designed to reduce risks to workers have become so expensive for employers to comply with that they may be counterproductive. Some employers have switched their defined benefit pension plans to money purchase (defined contribution) plans or have terminated them in favor of group RRSPs.

When a pension plan covers members in more than one province, the laws of each province apply to the members in that province. Likewise, if an employee has accrued benefits for work in more than one province, the laws of each province apply to the benefits accrued within that province, even for work within a single plan. Although U.S. pension law is complex, and is thought to be a factor in discouraging small firms from establishing defined benefit plans, the variation across provinces in Canada is an aspect of complexity not faced in the United States. Canadian federal and provincial regulators have made little progress towards uniform legislation.

The Pension Benefits Acts in the different provinces allow an employer to set up pension plans for distinct classes of employees (or to refrain from doing so). They, however, give all employees within a class for which a plan exists the right to join after two years of service (one year in Quebec). Part-time workers must be allowed to participate in the pension plan for their class, provided their earnings exceed a minimum amount. This treatment of part-time workers is more favorable than in the United States where plan sponsors may, and generally do, exclude part-time workers (working less than 1,000 hours a year) from their pension plans. The two-year vesting requirement is also more liberal than in the United States, where the requirement is five years. In these two respects—part-time workers and vesting—Canadian pension plans provide greater protection of workers than do U.S. plans. In the chapter on social security, it was similarly noted that Canadian workers with low service receive more favorable treatment from the social security system.

Employees' representatives have argued that pension contributions are deferred pay that should not be forfeited if the member dies. In line with this philosophy, some of the provincial Pension Benefits Acts provide for benefits to survivors in the case of preretirement death. In some provinces, the spouse of a member who dies in service after vesting is entitled to the full value of the member's deferred pension. In other provinces, the spouse must receive at least 60 percent of the value of the member's pension.

Private Pension Plans in the United States

Private pension plans in the United States have traditionally been predominantly defined benefit plans, but that situation has changed. In 1975, 72 percent of the assets in private sector employer-provided pension plans were in defined benefit plans. By 1996, that percentage fell to 51 percent, a decline on average of one percentage point per year over the 21-year period (U.S. Department of Labor 2000). Projecting the trend to the year 2000, less than half of pension assets in the United States were in defined benefit plans at the turn of the century.

The trend has been even more dramatic for participants. In 1975, 71 percent of active participants in pension plans were in defined benefit plans, roughly the same percentage as for assets. By 1996, only 34 percent of active participants were in defined benefit plans. The number of active participants in defined benefit plans has declined from a high of 30.2 million in 1984 to 23.3 million in 1996.

The growth of 401(k) plans has played a major role in the growth of defined contribution plans and the decline in defined benefit plans. 401(k) plans are defined contribution plans where employees as well as employers can make tax deductible contributions. These plans are named after the section of the Internal Revenue Code that enabled them. For other types of defined contribution plans, as well as for defined benefit plans, employees' contributions in the United States are not tax deductible.

A related trend is the growth of cash balance plans. Cash balance plans are one of the major innovations in pensions that occurred during the 1990s. Few firms sponsored them before the early 1990s, but a 1999 survey indicated that 19 percent of all Fortune 1000 firms sponsored them at the end of the decade (U.S. General Accounting Office 2000). These plans are legally classified as defined benefit plans because the value of promised benefits is not based on the value of actual plan assets, but they incorporate features of defined contribution plans. Each worker has a hypothetical account to which hypothetical contributions and hypothetical interest payments are credited.

From the perspective of workers, each worker has an individual account with an account balance. Each period, the employer contributes to the account on behalf of the worker. In these respects, cash balance plans are exactly like defined contribution plans. In cash balance plans, workers know the amount in the account, making it much easier to understand than traditional defined benefit plans, where it is difficult to determine the value of benefits accrued in mid career. For this reason, cash balance plans are like traditional defined contribution plans in that the benefits are portable for job changers.

In a typical defined benefit plan, workers face risks associated with the wage payments in their final years of work. Under a typical defined contribution plan, these risks are reduced because the benefit is based on wages over the entire career. In this respect, cash balance plans are like defined contribution plans.

Each period, interest is credited to the account. The interest rate may be guaranteed at a fixed level or may vary with the rate on a particular asset, such as 30-year Treasury bills. To the extent that the crediting rate varies with financial market conditions, workers bear financial market risk on their cash balance accounts, as do workers with defined contribution plans.

When interest rates vary, that causes capital gains or losses on holdings of bonds due to associated changes in bond prices. This type of financial market risk is not inherently an aspect of cash balance plans, and in this respect differs from defined contribution plans. However, as they are currently governed by pension regulation, the lump sum payment a worker would receive at termination may vary due to changes in interest rates because the lump-sum payment is calculated as the present value of the expected benefit at retirement. When the expected benefit at retirement is determined by a crediting rate that differs from the rate used to discount future benefits, workers will bear financial market risk due to capital gains of losses caused by interest rate changes on the present value of their pension benefits. In cash balance plans, workers may face interest rate risk at the time of retirement if they wish to annuitize their account balance. This risk is typical of defined contribution plans.

As well as participating in employer-provided plans, workers may also establish Individual Retirement Accounts for themselves. However, these plans are of little consequence for most workers because of the low maximum allowable annual contribution of $2,000.

Nearly half of all U.S. private sector employees participate in a retirement plan, and pension costs average 4.3 percent of payroll for plan sponsors (U.S. Chamber of Commerce 1992). In 1993, 49 percent of all wage and salary workers were covered by a pension plan. The coverage rate was 43 percent in the private sector and 77 percent in the public sector. Public sector pension participants accounted for about a quarter (27 percent) of all pension participants (U.S. Department of Labor 1994), far less than in Canada (48 percent).

THE TAX TREATMENT OF PENSIONS IN CANADA AND THE UNITED STATES

By providing favorable tax treatment to pensions as compared with other assets, Canadian and U.S. tax policies encourage firms to offer pension plans. Because of their proximity and the similarities in income and culture, it might be thought that the tax policy toward pensions of the two neighbors would be similar. In fact, important differences exist that may cause differences in their private pension systems.

In both Canada and the United States, the tax treatment of pensions from the employer perspective is the same. Employer contributions to a pension plan are treated similarly to wages—both are tax deductible under the corporate income tax. Investment earnings in pension funds accumulate tax free. Pension assets and liabilities are not taxed.[3]

Workers are not taxed at the time their employer contributes to a pension fund on their behalf. All distributions from pension funds to workers are taxable under the personal income tax. In Canada, retirees receive an annual tax credit for the first Can.$1,000 of pension income. Pension distributions in both countries are not subject to the social security payroll tax. Worker contributions are treated differently in the two countries, and are discussed later.

The tax system affects the role of pensions in the compensation of workers.[4] We examine how the tax treatment of pensions affects three aspects of pensions relating to risk bearing: 1) pension coverage rates, 2) the generosity of pension benefits, and 3) defined benefit versus defined contribution plans.[5]

Pension Coverage

The pension coverage rate is the percentage of the workforce participating in a pension plan. While the concept is simple, the ways coverage is measured differ considerably, producing wide variation in statistics.

Empirical comparisons of private sector workers in Canada and the United States are difficult because the distinction between the private sector and public sector is not as clear in Canada as it is in the United States. It appears that some public sector Canadian workers who work for institutions such as universities, hospitals, and public corporations (such as Air Canada), rather than traditional government bureaucracies, respond in household surveys that they are private sector workers. Because of this apparent misreporting, Canadian data for the entire workforce are more reliable than data that attempt to separate out private sector workers. However, because the public sector is relatively larger in Canada and because pension coverage rates are considerably higher in the public than the private sector, empirical comparisons across the two countries are difficult. In sum, the coverage rate for the entire workforce has the advantage that it indicates the percentage of the workforce in the two countries that has an employer-provided pension that supplements social security. It has the disadvantage that it is influenced by government policy concerning the relative size of the public sector.

Dailey and Turner (1992) attempted to measure private pension coverage on a comparable basis for Canada and the United States. That study found that, for many years, the private pension coverage rate has been about 50 percent higher in the United States than in Canada. Since 1975, the pension coverage rate for full-time private sector workers has varied between 28 and 30 percent in Canada, while it has varied between 44 and 46 percent in the United States.

Several problems cause those figures to overstate the difference in private sector coverage rates between the two countries. Since 1990 Statistics Canada has stated that it was not possible to accurately determine private sector pension coverage rates in Canada because of difficulties in determining who was in the private sector and that previous figures underestimated pension coverage. In addition, the U.S. figures are overstated because the Canadian figures are for the entire labor force, including the unemployed, while the U.S. figures are for wage and salary workers, excluding the unemployed. Adjusting for these problems, based on a subjective assessment of the magnitude of their effects, it would still appear that the private sector pension coverage rate was at least 5 percentage points higher in the United States.

Because of high coverage rates in the public sector and a higher relative amount of workers in the public sector, coverage rates for all workers, public and private sector, are higher in Canada for all income levels except the lowest, where the rate is marginally lower in Canada (Table 6.1). The coverage rates are 10–20 percentage points higher in the middle income categories, while the difference is only 4 percentage points in the highest income category.

The pension coverage of males has been declining in both Canada and the United States, while that of females has been increasing, presumably due to the increasing lifetime labor force participation of females. While in both countries the overall pension coverage rate has been fairly stable, in both it appears from the decline in male pension

Table 6.1 Pension Coverage Rates, by Income, All Workers (%)

Earnings (U.S.$)	Canada (1989)	United States (1993)
1 – 14,999	27	28
15,000 – 22,499	59	48
22,500 – 29,999	72	52
30,000 – 44,999	82	62
45,000 or more	73	69

SOURCE: Canada—Frenken and Maser (1992, p. 29); United States—unpublished tabulations from Current Population Survey Special Pension Supplement, 1993.

coverage rate that, holding constant employee work patterns, the probability of occupational pension coverage has decreased.

There has been a trend towards defined contribution plans in both countries. In Canada the membership in defined contribution plans increased from 8.4 percent of plan members in 1990 to 10.0 percent at the beginning of 1995.

Marginal income tax rates

In both countries, pension coverage rates increase with income, presumably at least partially because tax rates increase with income, but also because preferential tax treatment is worth more to individuals with high marginal income tax rates. If an individual's marginal income tax rate is the same in the preretirement and postretirement periods, then—in both Canada and the United States—the individual earns the pretax rate of return on pension saving. This occurs because the investment earnings on pension funds are untaxed. The incentive that the tax system provides for participating in a pension is thus higher with higher marginal income tax rates. The "wedge" between the pre-tax and the after-tax rate of return is higher in Canada for most workers because income tax rates are higher in Canada and the top rates are reached at lower levels of income.

Provincial tax rates differ in Canada but to a lesser extent than do state income tax rates (Alpert, Shoven, and Whalley 1992). About 40 percent of Canadian employees work in the province of Ontario, and thus Ontario is a major component of the Canadian experience. In 1996, the maximum tax rate—federal plus provincial—was 53 percent in Ontario (Table 6.2). This maximum rate was reached at a taxable income of $49,990. (Unless indicated otherwise, all amounts are expressed in U.S. dollars, at the exchange rate of U.S.$0.75 per Can.$1)

Marginal federal income tax rates were reduced in both countries during the 1980s. In Canada, the top rate was reduced from 65 percent in 1980 to 29 percent in 1987. It should be noted, however, that provincial income tax rates are much higher than state income tax rates. For this reason, comparing only marginal federal tax rates is misleading because the federal-provincial split of income tax is far different in Canada than the federal-state split is in the United States.

The highest marginal U.S. income tax rate on federal personal income taxes was 80 percent in 1980. The Tax Reform Act of 1986 reduced the top federal rate on wealthiest households to 28 percent. The highest rate was 33 percent and applied for some middle income taxpayers. Marginal tax rates have since risen. In 1994, the highest marginal federal income tax rate was 39.6 percent and applied to families with income above $250,000 (Table 6.2). In addition, taxpayers are liable for state income tax, which in some states reaches as high as 11 percent. Thus, the highest marginal income tax rate in the United

Table 6.2 Marginal Federal Plus Provincial or State Income Tax Rates in Canada and the United States[a] (%)

Family taxable income (U.S.$)	Canada (Province of Ontario)	United States (national average)
0 – 22,750	(up to) 27	19
22,750 – 55,100	(up to) 53	33
55,100 – 115,000	53	36
115,000 – 250,000	53	42
250,000 or more	53	46

[a] Provincial income tax rates are much higher in Canada than are state income tax rates in the United States. The average state income tax rates are calculated from the CPS Special Pension Supplement, April 1993 for the 1992 tax year. For the income brackets in the table, they are, respectively, 3.8%, 4.6%, 5.1%, and 5.9%. Because of top coding of income in the data, there is no income reported greater than $250,000. The average state income tax rate for the preceding category is used for the top income category in this table.

States (state plus federal rates) is currently 51 percent, but only the top few percent of families pay that rate. Workers with family income of $50,000 would pay, on average, a marginal tax rate (federal plus state) of about 33 percent and thus have marginal tax rates about 20 percentage points lower than in Canada.[6]

These comparisons do not include social security taxes. Social security is largely funded through general revenues in Canada, while it is funded by a payroll tax in the United States. When social security taxes are included, the share of social security and personal income taxes in GNP in 1987 was 18.0 percent in Canada and 19.5 percent in the United States (Wilson 1992). The social security payroll tax rate in Canada in 1999 was 7.0 percent, shared equally by employers and employees, compared to 12.4 percent in the United States. However, to the extent social security benefits are related to earnings, some workers may view the true social security tax rate as being lower than the statutory rate (Burkhauser and Turner 1985).

Empirical studies in the United States have shown that higher marginal income tax rates encourage the provision of pensions. In their study of pension coverage in 1979, 1988, and 1993, Reagan and Turner (1997) found that, on average, a one percentage point increase in marginal income tax rates increases pension coverage rates by 0.4 percentage points.[7] This finding suggests that, based solely on marginal income tax rates, pension coverage would be roughly 5–7 percentage points higher in Canada than in the United States.

Income tax progressivity

As well as being affected by the level of marginal income tax rates, the tax incentive for pensions is greater, with greater progressivity of the tax system. Workers generally have lower income in retirement than while working. With a more progressive tax system, the greater the reduction in income during retirement, the lower the marginal tax rate paid on pension benefits.

Because the highest marginal rate starts at a much lower income in Canada, marginal rates are more "compressed." It might therefore appear that higher income Canadians are less likely than Americans to face lower marginal rates in their retirement years than while working. In the United States, however, the tax system is also not very progressive but for a different reason. The top marginal bracket begins at a high income level, and a single marginal rate covers a wide range of the distribution of income. Reagan and Turner (1997) found, in their regression sample of males aged 21–55 in 1979, that the mean marginal tax rate (federal plus state) was 32 percent with a standard deviation of 13 percentage points. These figures had declined in 1993 to a marginal rate of 25 percent with a standard deviation of 9 percentage points. Thus, neither the Canadian nor the U.S. tax system is very progressive.

Tax subsidies for high-income workers

To examine further coverage rate differences between the two countries, we focus separately on the tax treatment of high- and low-income workers. The centerpiece of the 1991 tax reform in Canada is the establishment of a comprehensive limit to tax-assisted pension saving. All workers are permitted to contribute the lesser of 18 percent of their earned income (in the previous calendar year) or a maximum dollar amount (if lower) to a RRSP.

For individuals with relatively high incomes, the tax assistance provided to pension savings is considerably higher in the United States. In the late 1990s, the maximum compensation that could be used for calculating pension benefits that receive preferential tax treatment was more than twice as high in the United States than Canada.[8]

Some benefits consultants have argued that a low ceiling on compensation used for calculating pension benefits reduces the incentive for employers to provide pensions because the personal benefit to high-income employers is reduced. This argument is most likely to be valid for the owners of successful small firms, where the owner may weigh the amount that he or she can accumulate in a pension versus the cost of providing pensions to his or her employees. If this argument is valid, it may partially explain why pension coverage appears to be lower in the private sector in Canada than in the United States.

Beginning in 1984 in the United States, some higher income taxpayers have faced an implicit tax on their pension benefits in addition to the personal income tax. Up to 50 percent of social security benefits could be included in taxable income for persons with adjusted gross income plus certain nontaxable income above $25,000 for individuals and $32,000 for married couples. Under the 1993 Omnibus Budget Reconciliation Act, a two-tier tax liability was established, so that the proportion of benefits for retirees with income in the second-tier range was increased to 85 percent. Thus, at the margin for some workers, increases in pension benefits are taxed at the worker's marginal tax rate and cause the worker's social security benefits to become taxable. Eighteen percent of families with social security benefits pay taxes on those benefits, but more than half of families in the eighth, ninth, and tenth deciles are taxed (Pattison 1994). The net result is that many higher income workers pay an implicit tax on pension benefits of 20 to 40 percent due to the taxation of their social security benefits.

In sum, high-income workers in Canada face a greater tax incentive to invest in tax-sheltered assets than they do in the United States. However, the amount they can shelter through pensions is lower.

Implicit taxes on low-income workers

In addition to explicit taxes, implicit taxes may also reduce the net receipt of pension benefits. For Canadians with low lifetime earnings, the income-tested component of the social security system discourages participation in an employer-sponsored pension plan. All Canadians aged 65 and over, independent of their work history, receive a small flat rate OAS benefit. Canadians with no other source of income also receive income-tested benefits from the Guaranteed Income Supplement (GIS). For each dollar of retirement income above the flat rate OAS benefits, GIS benefits are reduced by 50 cents.

The maximum pension payable from the earnings-related component of Canada's public retirement system, the Canada Pension Plan (CPP), was based on maximum preretirement earnings of Can.$37,400 a year in 1999. An individual receiving the maximum CPP benefit would still qualify for partial GIS benefits if the individual had no other retirement income than the flat rate OAS benefits. So, too, would individuals not entitled to the maximum CPP benefit.

The net result is that Canadians with low lifetime earnings face a 50 percent tax rate on private pension income during retirement, in addition to federal and provincial income taxes. These public pension provisions, in effect since 1966, provide a strong disincentive for low-income workers to participate in an employer-sponsored pension plan.[9] A similar disincentive exists in the United States due to the income testing for eligibility for Supplemental Security Income, but that program only effects very low income workers.

Individual pension plans

The Canadian government has set contribution limits for money purchase plans and RRSP equivalent to the limits for defined benefit plans. The federal tax rules treat employers and employees the same, regardless of the type of pension plan.

A primary objective of the Canadian tax treatment of pensions is to provide equitable tax assistance for retirement, regardless of whether a worker participates in a company-sponsored pension plan or in an individual account pension plan. In Canada, workers setting up RRSPs can access approximately the same amount of tax assistance as do workers participating in employer-provided plans.

In the United States, no attempt has been made to equalize the treatment between employer-sponsored plans and individual plans. Employers in the United States have a near monopoly in the provision of tax-favored pension benefits. Since 1981, the maximum an individual can deduct for contributions to an Individual Retirement Account (IRA) has been frozen at $2,000.[10] Inflation has more than halved the real value of this tax deduction. The amount that can be contributed to personal pension plans is only a small percentage of what can be contributed to employer sponsored plans, while in Canada the amounts are equal.

Registered Retirement Savings Plans also enjoy other advantages over IRAs. Since tax reform in 1990, failure to contribute to a RRSP by the deadline does not cause the deduction to be lost. Unused contribution amounts may be carried forward, subject to a seven-year limit, and deducted when made. No such carry-forward provision exists for IRAs.

Since 1990, there is no tax advantage to participating in an employer-provided plan since an equal amount could be contributed to an RRSP. This change should cause a reduction in pension coverage rates in Canada, with employer-provided plans being replaced by individual account plans. However, a study of data previous to that change found no negative relationship between the amount of employer-provided pension assets held by an individual and their RRSP assets (Venti and Wise 1994). In 1987, for example, 37 percent of tax filers who contributed to a pension plan also contributed to an RRSP versus only

16 percent of tax filers who did not contribute to a pension plan (Frenken 1990).

Summary

In sum, the higher marginal income tax rates in Canada would—other things equal—cause pension coverage rates to be roughly 5–7 percentage points higher than in the United States. This effect may be offset somewhat by higher social security tax rates in the United States. An explanation for relatively lower pension coverage rates at lower income levels is that the income-tested provisions of the Canadian social security system place an implicit tax of 50 percent on the pension benefits of workers with low lifetime earnings.

Other explanations

Other factors besides taxes affect pension coverage. Social security is moderately more generous in Canada than in the United States, which would lower pension benefit levels and probably also pension coverage rates in Canada. The United States, through nondiscrimination rules, requires employers that offer pensions to offer them to most of their full-time employees. This regulation is one way that public policy attempts to expand coverage. Canada has no such regulation.

Since 1987 in most provinces in Canada, pension benefits are locked in after vesting, and workers cannot access those benefits until retirement. In the United States, workers can take a lump sum distribution from their pension plan when they change jobs if the plan permits it. It has been argued in the United States that prohibiting preretirement lump sum distributions would reduce pension coverage because it would reduce the flexibility that workers have to use those funds for nonretirement purposes.

The Generosity of Pension Plans

While pension coverage measures one dimension of the extent that pension plans provide an element of risk bearing concerning retirement income, the generosity of pension plans measures another dimension. One measure of pension plan generosity is the level of pension benefits being paid to current retirees. The level of pension benefits, however, does not directly measure the generosity of pension benefit formulas because other factors also affect benefit levels. For example, if a pension system is immature, workers having participated in it for less than their full career, it will pay lower retirement benefits than an equally generous system that is fully mature. While it is not evident that the Canadian and U.S. pension systems differ in their maturities, such a difference could cause average benefit levels to differ.

Canadian private pension plans have been slightly less generous than U.S. private plans in the level of benefits they provide. Canadian pensions in the late 1980s provided slightly less and U.S. pensions provided slightly more than $6,000 in annual benefits (Dailey and Turner 1992).

Canada and the United States differ considerably in the maximum amount that a worker can save through the pension system. In Canada, the maximum percentage of earnings that a worker can save is lower and, as indicated earlier, the maximum earnings that can be used in determining pension benefits is much lower.

The maximum limit in Canada for contributions to a defined contribution plan is 18 percent of worker earnings. In Canada, the maximum benefit for a defined benefit plan is the lesser of $45,185 per year or 70 percent of the participants earnings in the three highest years.

Both the defined contribution and defined benefit limits are higher in the United States. The maximum contributions to a defined contribution plan in 1997 was 25 percent of earnings for most workers, and for workers earning more than $120,000 a year it was $30,000. For a defined benefit plan, the maximum benefit was the lesser of $125,000 a year or 100 percent of the participant's average compensation for his or her three highest-earnings years. For high-income workers, the maximum pension benefit in Canada is less than half as large as in the United States.

The lower maximum contributions and benefits in Canada, however, may be of little economic significance if few workers are constrained by the limits. The difference is most likely to be constraining for older workers and higher income workers who, because of the ceiling on social security benefits, are more likely to wish to save a relatively large fraction of their income for retirement.

If the 18 percent maximum is not a binding constraint in that most workers save less, the higher marginal income tax rates in Canada would encourage middle income workers to save more in pensions than they do in the United States.

Defined Benefit versus Defined Contribution Plans

An employer's first decision when considering pension risk is whether to provide a defined benefit or defined contribution plan or both. In both the United States and Canada, defined contribution plans have grown at the expense of defined benefit plans.

In the United States, there has been a major shift from defined benefit plans towards defined contribution plans. While the number of active participants in defined benefit plans was nearly 4 million lower in 1995 than in 1975, the number in defined contribution plans grew by 31 million, due to the growth of 401(k) plans (U.S. Department of Labor 2000).

There has also been a trend towards defined contribution plans in Canada, but the trend has been much weaker. Between 1982 and 1995, for example, the percentage of pension participants who belonged to money purchase plans rose from 5.3 percent to 10.0 percent, while the percentage who belonged to defined benefit plans declined from 93.7 to 88.6 percent.[11]

If defined benefit plan assets in the United States were the same percentage of pension assets in 1995 that they were in 1975, there would have been $500 billion less in defined contribution assets and the same amount more in defined benefit assets. This works out to be roughly $6,000 less in defined benefit assets per participant in the private pension system. Because of backloading of defined benefit pensions and the accrual of benefits with greater job tenure, this number would be higher for older workers and lower for younger workers. If the implicit insurance premium that firms charge workers for providing defined benefit plans rather than defined contribution plans were a couple of percentage points of assets, older workers covered by defined benefit plans have lost several hundred dollars a year in implicit insurance value from the switch from defined benefit to defined contribution plans.

In defined contribution plans, workers bear market risk to the extent that the plans are invested in risky assets. In defined benefit plans, workers bear firm specific risks relating to the viability of the firm. In financially strong firms, defined contribution plans are riskier for workers than defined benefit plans. By switching from defined benefit to defined contribution plans in this situation, the firm is transferring risk from the shareholders to the workers. The workers should be willing to bear this risk if they are compensated for it. It is likely, however, that shareholders have a greater capacity for risk bearing than do workers. Shareholders can diversify firm specific risk more easily (by investing in other firms) than can workers, for whom firm specific risk to earnings affects a large part of income-producing capacity.

Clark and McDermed (1990) ascribe most of the shift towards defined contribution plans in the United States to changes in pension policy that have made defined contribution plans relatively less costly to provide than defined benefit plans. Gustman and Steinmeier (1992), however, argue that the dominant factor has been structural changes in the economy—the relative decline in traditionally strong defined benefit sectors of unionized and manufacturing employment. Both factors have doubtlessly played a role, with their relative importance being less clear.

It is commonly thought that defined contribution plans, where investment risk work is borne by the worker, entail greater risk to workers than do defined benefit plans, where investment risk is borne by the employer. The comparison is more complex, however.   Inflation risk may be lower in defined contribution plans than in defined benefit plans that do not provide postretirement cost-of-living adjustments, which is frequently the case in small defined benefit plans. Workers may bear some investment risk in defined benefit plans if those plans adjust their generosity or are more likely to provide cost-of-living adjustments when they have favorable investment returns.[12]

The loss of a job has more serious consequences with regard to defined benefit pension benefits for an older worker than it does for a younger worker. Because defined benefit pensions are based on the worker's terminal nominal earnings in most plans, a worker who loses his job in his late 40s suffers a large loss in future pension benefits because inflation erodes the real value of his earnings used to calculate his pension benefits. Mobile workers bear less job-change risk in defined contribution plans than in defined benefit plans because, once vested, the value of future benefits is not reduced by job change in defined contribution plans while, with the exception of cash benefit plans, it generally is in defined benefit plans (Turner 1993).

Tax reform in Canada, implemented in 1990, seeks to "level the playing field" with regard to the tax assistance provided to pension saving in different types of plans. The maximum amount of tax assistance provided to members of employer-sponsored defined benefit and defined contribution plans, as well as to RRSPs, is intended to be equal. Further, through the introduction of a new carry-forward provision, individuals are provided with greater flexibility in the timing of RRSP contributions. This provision was enacted to give defined contribution plans the flexibility afforded defined benefit plans because firms who sponsor defined benefit plans can make retroactive enrichments of their plans.

In Canada, the 18 percent maximum allowable contribution to a defined contribution plan was chosen because it is roughly equivalent to the defined benefit limit. The defined benefit limit is 2 percent of final earnings per year of service, with a maximum of 70 percent of highest earnings (Wyatt 1990).

In the United States, the defined benefit limit does not vary with years of service, as it does in Canada. The maximum benefit that can be received from a defined contribution plan, in both Canada and the United States, necessarily increases with service because the maximum benefit is based on the accumulation of contributions and investment earnings over time. Because the U.S. limit does not vary with service, short-service workers in the United States can receive higher benefits through a defined benefit plan than they can through a defined contribution plan. For long-service workers, the situation is the reverse.

Within its lower contribution limits, Canada allows individuals greater flexibility in the timing of their contributions. In Canada, an individual's unused contribution allowance in each year is carried forward indefinitely for use in subsequent years, subject to certain dollar limits. Similarly, contributions not deductible in the year in which they are paid may be deducted in subsequent years.

In the United States, contributions not deductible in the year paid are subject to a 10 percent excise tax. Before 1987, a credit carry-forward was available when an employer's contributions to a profit sharing plan were less than the maximum allowed (McGill and Grubbs 1989, p. 652). That carry-forward is no longer available. Flexibility is provided, however, by the higher limit on contributions, so it is not clear which system effectively provides the greater flexibility.

In the United States, employee contributions are only tax deductible for defined contribution plans, and then only for contributions to 401(k) plans. This feature of the tax code may favor these plans. In Canada, employee contributions are tax deductible to defined benefit plans as well as defined contribution plans.

The tax benefit of overfunding defined benefit plans

In assessing why employers might prefer defined benefit rather than defined contribution plans, financial economists (Tepper 1981; Black 1980) have drawn attention to the tax advantages to shareholders of overfunding such plans. In the United States, the Omnibus Reconciliation Act of 1987 (OBRA) reduced the desirability of defined benefit plans relative to defined contribution plans by reducing the amount that could be contributed to overfunded defined benefit plans (Ippolito 1990).

Under the OBRA rules, employer contributions are not tax deductible if the plan is overfunded by 50 percent on a termination basis. This reduced the flexibility firms have in managing defined benefit plans, and it reduced the amount that can be sheltered from tax. Termination liabilities are calculated as if the plan were to terminate immediately. For plans with a typical age structure of workers, these liabilities are considerably less than the liabilities calculated assuming that the plan will continue in existence. Those liabilities for ongoing plans recognize that currently accruing benefits are based on future wages, in final average pay plans. Under the OBRA rules, many defined benefit plans are not able to contribute sufficient amounts to a pension plan to cover the current accrual of liabilities. This creates a tax disadvantage for defined benefit plans because, by comparison, firms can contribute equal to the full current accrual of liabilities in defined contribution plans.

In Canada, too, the tax authorities seek to limit the amount of overfunding in defined benefit plans. However, the restrictions are less onerous than those in the United States. In Canada, employer contributions are tax deductible so long as the surplus in the plan is no more than 10 percent of actual plan liabilities or twice the annual value of current service contributions. However, the plan's liabilities are not valued on a termination basis for the purpose of this calculation. If the plan has a history of cost-of-living or similar adjustments, these may be taken into account in determining the plan's liability if it is reasonable to assume that such adjustments will continue. These adjustments would include, for example, *ad hoc* increases for pensioners and increases in accrued benefits under career average earnings plans and flat benefit plans. In Canada, a potentially more important constraint on the extent of overfunding is the uncertainty that may exist as to the ownership of surplus assets.

Summary

In Canada, an effort has been made to equalize the treatment of defined benefit and defined contribution plans. As a result, employee contributions are tax deductible for both defined benefit and defined contribution plans, while they are only tax deductible to one type of defined contribution plan in the United States. Defined benefit plans also receive more favorable tax treatment in Canada than they do in the United States in terms of allowable maximum funding. Greater flexibility is allowed for contributions to defined contribution plans in Canada than in the United States in order to try to equalize the degree of flexibility that employers and employees have to contribute to both types of plans. On balance, tax policy in Canada is relatively more favorable to defined benefit plans than it is in the United States. Perhaps, in part for that reason, defined benefit plans are relatively more prevalent in Canada.

COMPARISON OF THE RISK BEARING ASPECTS OF THE CANADIAN AND U.S. OCCUPATIONAL PENSION SYSTEMS

The Canadian and U.S. pension systems can be compared in terms of several aspects of risk bearing.

Early Retirement Insurance

Many defined benefit RPP beneficiaries in Canada who take early retirement receive a supplementary benefit, called a bridging benefit, from the time of retirement until age 65 (Frenken 1995). This type of benefit is also provided by some U.S. defined benefit plans, but it is not available from defined contribution plans in either country.

Pension Insurance

The use of pension insurance is a major difference between the pension systems of Canada and the United States. The United States insures defined benefit pension benefits through the Pension Benefit Guaranty Corporation (PBGC). Canada, with the exception of one province (Ontario), does not insure pension benefits. Does this difference imply that defined benefit pension benefits are less risky in the United States? Not necessarily, because Canada reduces pension benefit risks through regulations that assure that defined benefit plans will be adequately funded.

Ontario's Pension Benefit Guaranty Fund (PBGF) became operational in 1983, to cover part of accrued benefits of private defined benefit plans. Premiums initially consisted of 0.2 percent of the unfunded liability reported by the sponsor. Policymakers realized this was a poor measure of the risk to the insurance fund. Ontario subsequently modified the premium structure to include an annual charge of Can.$1 per active participant or beneficiary and a sliding scale for the annual risk-adjusted component. The scale increases to 1.5 percent of unfunded liabilities for larger unfunded liabilities. Unlike the maximum benefit guaranteed by the PBGC in the United States, which is price indexed, the maximum guaranteed benefit of Can.$1,000 per month has not been increased since the program's inception and thus has considerably eroded in real value due to inflation. The maximum guaranteed benefit is now about one-third the level of the maximum guaranteed benefit in the United States. In addition, there are qualifying restrictions that do not apply in the United States. A terminated worker must be at least 45 years old with 10 years of service when terminated to be covered by the insurance. For active employees, their sum of age and years of service must total more than 55.

The PBGC in the United States acts like a pension safety net for most participants in defined benefit plans. It prevents the devastating loss of pension benefits that occurred in the early 1970s with the bankruptcy of some firms. Often, firms that have become bankrupt and have defined benefit pensions have underfunded their pensions. Underfunding formerly was a concern for workers in firms that were financially weak. The PBGC provides workers with the assurance that payment of their pension is no longer entirely dependent on their employer's financial health.

The PBGC does not guarantee all benefits, and most workers do not receive what they would have received from their plan had it continued in existence. It guarantees what it considers to be basic benefits. These include the vested benefits of people age 65 and older that have been in effect for five years or longer—up to a limit, which increases each year with inflation. In 1995, the annual limit was $30,886 for workers age 65. The cap is lower for younger workers. Other guaranteed benefits include survivor's annuity benefits.

Legislative reforms were enacted in 1994 in the Retirement Protection Act. While there once was concern about adequacy of the funding of PBGC, with the legislative changes that have improved both PBGC's funding and the funding of the plans it insures, it has sufficient assets to cover anticipated benefit payments for many years.

CONCLUSIONS

It appears that, in both Canada and the United States, the probability of pension coverage given worker characteristics has declined, indicating that risk sharing through pensions has declined. Furthermore, defined benefit coverage has declined and defined contribution coverage has increased in both countries. These changes have increased the risks borne by long-term employees but have decreased the risk for job-changing employees. In the United States, most defined benefit plan participants are covered by pension benefit insurance, which is not the case in Canada. Overall, it appears that risk bearing has increased for workers in both Canada and the United States due to changes in the occupational pension systems in the two countries.

Notes

1. This study used the 1988 purchasing power parity of Can.$1 equals U.S.$0.80. We use the slightly lower value of U.S.$0.75 for making comparisons.
2. The lower average social security benefits in the United States may arise in part because more older Americans are working and not receiving social security benefits.
3. In the United States, premium payments to the Pension Benefit Guaranty Corporation are based on the unfunded liabilities of pension plans. This is also true for the Guarantee Fund in Ontario. We are not considering these levies as taxes.
4. Generally, a tax policy affecting a worker's decisions distorts economic activity from what it would have been without taxes. However, in a system with multiple taxes, one aspect of taxation may correct distortions introduced by another aspect. The optimality of pension tax policy in terms of creating or correcting distortions is not discussed here (Ippolito 1990).
5. We thus do not discuss, for example, the effects of taxation of pensions on income distribution, government revenues, or the capital market.
6. The higher marginal personal income taxes in Canada are reflected in personal income taxes being about 25 percent larger as a percentage of GNP in Canada than in the United States (Wilson 1992).
7. The marginal effect is probably lower at higher tax rates. See also Woodbury (1983), Woodbury and Bettinger (1991), and Woodbury and Huang (1991).
8. An explanation for the more favorable tax treatment for pensions of high-income workers in the United States than in Canada may be that, with its higher income inequality, there are relatively more high-income workers in the United States, and therefore they presumably have more political power.
9. This issue has important implications, as well, for public policy. In Canada, the fact that pension coverage is far from universal is often cited by critics as proof of the inadequacy of the private pension system and the need, therefore, to expand the public pension system or to mandate private pension coverage. (In 1995, 45.3 percent of males and 44.1 percent of females who were paid workers belonged to an occupational pension plan [Statistics Canada 1996].) However, the absence of universal coverage is perhaps best seen as a statement about workers' revealed preferences rather than as a "failure" of the private pension system.

   The introduction of a mandatory private pension plan—inclusive of part-time as well as full-time workers—is likely to reduce the lifetime resources available to those with low lifetime earnings. The incidence of employer contributions to a mandatory private pension plan (if it is not retroactive) is likely to fall ultimately on the employee. Workers, including those with low lifetime earnings, will be required to allocate a larger fraction of their lifetime earnings to provide for their retirement years. On one hand, this will gradually reduce the likelihood of future claims on income-tested programs such as GIS. On the other hand, by forcing persons with low lifetime earnings to provide a larger share of their own retirement incomes, this proposal may redistribute income away from those with low lifetime earnings.

In this context, two facts merit note. First, persons whose current earnings are low are less likely to be members of occupational pension plans. To the extent that current earnings are positively correlated with lifetime earnings, this fact suggests that those with low lifetime earnings are less likely to be covered by an occupational pension plan. Second, Canadians with low current incomes generally choose not to contribute to RRSPs. Given the low value to them of the tax subsidy associated with RRSP contributions together with the likelihood that they would be substituting their own savings for retirement for benefits available from income-tested public programs, this decision is probably rational.

10. The amount is $2,500 for a worker whose spouse does not also contribute to an IRA.

11. These figures do not add to 100 percent due to the presence of "composite and other plans."

12. For a discussion of how participants in defined benefit plans may bear at least some of the investment risk of the pension fund, see Hyatt and Pesando (1997). In a unionized firm, for example, poor fund performance may require the employer to make additional plan contributions. In this event, the employer may seek wage or other concessions in the next round of collective bargaining.

References

Alpert, William T., John B. Shoven, and John Whalley. 1992. "Introduction." In *Canada–U.S. Tax Comparisons,* John B. Shoven and John Whalley, eds. Chicago, Illinois: University of Chicago Press, pp. 1–24.

Black, Fischer. 1980. "The Tax Consequences of Long Run Pension Policy." *Financial Analysts Journal* 36(July/August): 17–23.

Burkhauser, Richard V., and John A. Turner. 1985. "Is the Social Security Payroll Tax a Tax?" *Public Finance Quarterly* 13(July): 253–267.

Clark, Robert L., and Anne A. McDermed. 1990. *The Choice of Pension Plans in a Changing Regulatory Environment.* Washington, D.C.: American Enterprise Institute.

Dailey, Lorna M., and John A. Turner. 1992. "U.S. Pensions in World Perspective, 1970–1989." In *Trends in Pensions 1992,* John A. Turner and Daniel J. Beller, eds. Washington, D.C.: U.S. Government Printing Office.

Frenken, Hubert. 1990. "RRSPs: Tax-Assisted Retirement Savings." *Perspectives on Labour and Incomes* 2(Winter): 9–20.

_____. 1995. "Pension Plan Potpourri." *Perspectives on Labour and Income* 7(Summer): 20–27.

Frenken, Hubert, and Karen Maser. 1992. "Employer-Sponsored Pension Plans—Who is Covered?" *Perspectives on Labour and Income* 4(Winter): 27–34.

Gustman, Alan L., and Thomas L. Steinmeier. 1992. "The Stampede Toward Defined Contribution Plans: Fact or Fiction?" *Industrial and Labor Relations Review* 31(Spring): 361–369.

Hyatt, Douglas, and James E. Pesando. 1997. "Do Employees Actually Bear the Investment Risk in Defined Benefit Pension Plans?" *Canadian Labour & Employment Law* 5: 125–138.

Ippolito, Richard A. 1990. *An Economic Appraisal of Pension Tax Policy in the United States.* Homewood, Illinois: Irwin.

Maser, Karen. 1995. "Who's Saving for Retirement?" *Perspectives on Labour and Income* 7(Winter): 14–19.

McGill, Dan M., and Donald S. Grubbs, Jr. 1989. *Fundamentals of Private Pensions.* Sixth ed. Philadelphia: University of Pennsylvania Press.

Pattison, David. 1994. "Taxation of Social Security Benefits Under the New Income Tax Provisions: Distributional Estimates for 1994." *Social Security Bulletin* 57(Summer): 44–50.

Payne, Jennifer. 1997. "Pension Plans in Canada." *The Daily*, Statistics Canada, Ottawa, August 22.

Reagan, Patricia B., and John A. Turner. 1997. "Measuring the Sensitivity of Pension Coverage Rates to Changes in Marginal Tax Rates." *Proceedings*, National Tax Association, January.

Statistics Canada. 1996. *Pension Plans in Canada 1995.* Ottawa: Statistics Canada.

Tepper, Irwin. 1981. "Taxation and Corporate Pension Policy." *Journal of Finance* 36(March): 1–13.

Turner, John A. 1993. *Pension Policy for a Mobile Labor Force.* Kalamazoo, Michigan: W.E. Upjohn Institute for Employment Research.

U.S. Chamber of Commerce. 1992. *Employee Benefits 1991.* Washington, D.C.: U.S. Chamber of Commerce.

U.S. Department of Labor. 1994. *Abstract of the Form 5500.* Washington, D.C.: U.S. Department of Labor.

_____. 2000. *Abstract of the Form 5500.* Washington, D.C.: U.S. Department of Labor.

U.S. General Accounting Office. 2000. *Cash Balance Plans: Implications for Retirement Income.* Report USGAO/HEHS-00-207.

Venti, Steven F., and David A. Wise. 1994. "RRSPs and Saving in Canada." Working paper, National Bureau of Economic Research, Cambridge, Massachusetts.

Wilson, Thomas A. 1992. "Reflections on Canada–U.S. Tax Differences." In *Canada–U.S. Tax Comparisons*, John B. Shoven and John Whalley, eds. Chicago, Illinois: University of Chicago Press, pp. 365–374.

Wolfson, Michael C., and Brian B. Murphy. 1994. "Kinder and Gentler: A Comparative Analysis of Incomes of the Elderly in Canada and the United States." In *Economic Security and Intergenerational Justice: A Look at North America*, Theodore R. Marmor, Timothy M. Smeeding, and Vernon L. Greene, eds. Washington, D.C.: The Urban Institute Press, pp. 252–261.

Woodbury, Stephen A. 1983. "Substitution between Wage and Nonwage Benefits." *American Economic Review* 73(March): 166–182.

Woodbury, Stephen A., and Douglas R. Bettinger. 1991. "The Decline of Fringe-Benefit Coverage in the 1980s." In *Structural Changes in U.S. Labor Markets: Causes and Consequences,* Randall W. Eberts and Erica L. Groshen, eds. Armonk, New York: M.E. Sharpe, pp. 105–138.

Woodbury, Stephen A., and Wei-Jang Huang. 1991. *The Tax Treatment of Fringe Benefits.* Kalamazoo, Michigan: W.E. Upjohn Institute for Employment Research.

Wyatt Company. 1990. *Special Memorandum.* Toronto, Ontario: The Wyatt Company.

7
Risk Shifting
in Workers' Compensation

Douglas E. Hyatt

INTRODUCTION

When workers' compensation was introduced into North America in the early years of the twentieth century, it represented a significant departure for the workplace parties. In the 1800s, workers who sought compensation for injuries suffered in the workplace had to sue their employers in common law courts. Employers received substantial protection in the courts from three lines of defence. The first, called the "doctrine of contributory risk," allowed that, even if a marginal lack of care by the worker in the performance of their duties somehow contributed to the occurrence of the accident, then the worker was ineligible for compensation. Second, the "fellow servant doctrine" protected the employer from liability if the accident was a result of negligence by a fellow worker. Finally, the "doctrine of the assumption of risk" held that workers should reasonably be aware of the risks of a particular job and are presumed to have voluntarily assumed the risk if they accept the offer of employment. Further, workers were presumed to be paid a wage premium for accepting the higher degree of risk of a workplace injury, and the risk premium represented compensation for a potential accident. What data that are available from the before workers' compensation suggest that workers who went to court over work-related injuries experienced very limited success (Fishback and Kantor 1995).

In response to the devastating financial impacts felt by injured workers and their families under this regime, and mounting social unrest associated with other negative outcomes of the industrial revolution, politicians of the day began to enact legislation intended to weaken the defences of employers. As employers started to lose more cases, and as workers began to recognize that tort reforms would be insufficient to resolve the problems of compensation through the courts (e.g., delays, high costs and uncertainty about the outcome), support began to grow for an "automatic" compensation system. Even labor unions, which had traditionally opposed automatic compensation as a challenge to the role of unions to negotiate benefits for workers rather than have them mandated by governments, warmed to more comprehensive reforms.

In 1911, after a number of false starts and a series of constitutional challenges, the modern era of workers' compensation in North America commenced with the passage of the first comprehensive legislation in Wisconsin. Workers' compensation was introduced to Canada in 1914 when the first workers' compensation statute was passed by the Ontario legislature. In order to deflect constitutional challenges, most of which were based upon the argument that workers' compensation deprived employers of their property without due process of law, U.S. legislation contained a number of design features that remain prevalent to this day. These include incomplete coverage of all workers, benefit levels subject to statutory maximums, benefits determined as a function of earnings, and waiting periods following the injury before benefits are payable. Since Canadian workers' compensation legislation was based heavily on U.S. statutes, particularly the Washington State law, many of these features exist across all North American jurisdictions.

In essence, workers' compensation is a mandatory, employer-financed, no-fault insurance scheme that pays the costs of medical treatment, vocational rehabilitation, and indemnity benefits associated with lost earnings due to work-related injuries and diseases. The existence of a workers' compensation system is often heralded as an historic *quid pro quo* between employers and workers. In return for benefits paid with certainty, regardless of fault, workers ceded the right to sue their employers for work-related injuries.

As the nature of the employment relationship, work, and the workplace have changed since the early 1900s, the workers' compensation system has struggled to adapt. Globalization has intensified pressures on product, capital, and labor markets. Together, these related forces have altered the demands on the workers' compensation system. This chapter considers the question of whether the "historic compromise" is eroding, with a particular focus on the extent to which the risks of workplace injuries and illness are being shifted more directly onto workers.

The chapter proceeds as follows. The next section provides a basic overview of workers' compensation in the United States and Canada. The third section reviews the economic theory on the incidence of workers' compensation costs and summarizes the empirical research which suggests that at least part of these costs are passed on to workers in the form of lower wages. The current climate of workers' compensation is then described. The fifth section suggests a number of consequences of workers' compensation reform efforts that have the impact of shifting the financial burden of workplace injuries and illnesses more directly onto individual workers. The chapter concludes with summary comments.

A BRIEF OVERVIEW OF WORKERS' COMPENSATION

Unlike most other industrialized nations which have national programs, legislative authority for workers' compensation is delegated to the state/province (and in some instances, sectoral) level in North America. There are 58 workers' compensation jurisdictions in the United States and 13 in Canada. The basic functions of workers' compensation are the provision of medical rehabilitation, payment of indemnity benefits based upon the severity of the injury, provision of vocational rehabilitation services when appropriate, and the creation of incentives to improve health and safety, usually through experience rating employer workers' compensation insurance premiums. The details of how these functions are accomplished vary considerably across jurisdictions. The description of workers' compensation that follows offers only some generalizations about the dimensions of the system. Readers who are interested in more detail should refer to the Association of Workers' Compensation Boards of Canada (1993), United States Chamber of Commerce (various years), and U.S. Department of Labor (1996, 1997), Spieler (1994), Spieler and Burton (1998), Larson and Larson (1998), and Mont, Burton, and Reno (1999).

Although workers' compensation is a mandated program, the proportion of workers covered by the legislation varies considerably by jurisdiction. In the United States, about 98.6 percent of private sector workers and 99.8 percent of state and local government employees are covered by workers' compensation (Mont, Burton, and Reno 1999). In Canada, approximately 81 percent of workers are covered, ranging from about 70 percent of workers in Ontario to in excess of 95 percent of workers in British Columbia, Quebec, and Yukon. Most jurisdictions specify some exemptions from coverage based on industry and/or occupation. Examples of common exclusions in Canada include the self-employed (or independent contractors), domestics, outworkers (persons who perform their employment tasks in their homes), professional athletes, small firms, casual or seasonal employees, farm laborers, volunteers and nonprofit organizations, independent truckers, teachers, clergy, and, in some jurisdictions, banks and other financial institutions.

Workers' compensation pays three broad types of indemnity benefits—temporary disability benefits, permanent disability benefits, and death benefits. *Temporary disability* benefits compensate workers for loss of employment income until the insured worker fully recovers, until the point in time beyond which the worker is unlikely to experience any significant further recovery, or (in some jurisdictions) until a specific time limit (e.g., 104 weeks) has expired. Most U.S. jurisdictions pay 60–66 percent of (gross) earnings, up to some maximum benefit level. Half a dozen states pay benefits based on net or take-home earnings. In Canada, temporary total disability benefits range from 70 percent of gross earnings to 90 percent of net earnings, also up to some maximum level.

Those workers who do not fully recover their time-of-injury health status but are instead left with a residual physical impairment may be eligible for *permanent disability* benefits. There is considerable variation in the formulas for permanent disability benefits across North American workers' compensation jurisdictions, but they are typically based on lost earnings, functional impairment, or some combination of the two. In some instances, benefits are also paid to indemnify lost retirement income.[1] In the case of Ontario, for example, an additional sum equal to 10 percent of a workers' permanent disability award is deposited into a money purchase pension fund administered by the Workers' Compensation Board. When the worker reaches age 65, the permanent disability benefit ceases, and an annuity is purchased with contributions and accrued returns on account of the worker. The annuity pays a retirement benefit until the worker's death.

Death benefits are paid to the spouses and, in some instances, the dependents of a worker who is fatally injured at work or who dies from a disease recognized by the workers' compensation system as being attributable to work. Benefits can include lump-sum payments, pensions, funeral expenses, and allowances for vocational training and/or counseling for the surviving spouse.

Figures 7.1 and 7.2 show the rates per 100 workers of total and lost-time injuries and illnesses (i.e., injuries and illnesses which require the worker to miss at least one day of work beyond the date of injury) over the period of 1972–1996 for the United States and Canada, respectively. While it is difficult to compare the numbers across countries due to myriad definitional differences, the figures do permit an examination of basic trends. In the United States, after reaching a high of 11 claims per 100 workers in 1973, the total claims rate fell slowly over the next decade. Since 1987, the incidence of claims has fallen in the range of 8.3–8.9 per 100 workers. There was a considerable reduction to 7.4 claims per 100 workers in 1996. The lost-time claims rate in the United States was fairly stable in the 3.5–4.0 range until the 1990s. During the 1990s, the lost-time claims rate trended down.[2]

In Canada, the total claims frequency rate has dropped markedly from the levels experienced in the 1970s and early 1980s, when the rate fell between 10 and 13 per 100 workers. Since 1985, the frequency of claims has fallen from 10.7 per 100 workers to 6.5 per 100 workers in 1996. During the 1985–1996 period, the frequency of lost-time injuries also fell, from 5.7 to 3.1 claims per 100 workers.

In Canada in 1996, 785,666 workers' compensation claims were reported. Of these, 379,554 resulted in the worker losing at least one day of work. In the United States, there were some 6.2 million injuries of which 1.9 million resulted in lost time from work.

Workers' compensation insurance is provided in Canada through a monopoly provincial or territorial Workers' Compensation Board. In contrast, workers' compensation insurance in the United States is provided through various organizational structures: a monopoly board (six states); combinations of state and private carriers (19 states); and private carriers exclusively (25 states).

Figure 7.1 Workers' Compensation Claims Incidence Rates, United States, 1972–1996 (per 100 workers)

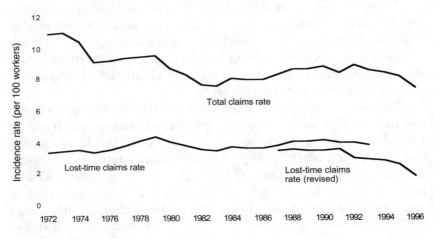

SOURCE: Burton and Schmidle (1996).

Figure 7.2 Workers' Compensation Claims Incidence Rates, Canada, 1972–1996 (per 100 workers),

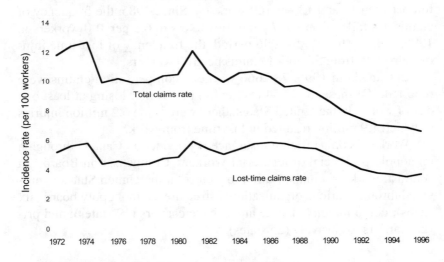

SOURCE: Human Resources Development Canada (1997).

While the workers' compensation system in North America follows the spirit of the German system that arose under Bismarck in the 1880s, it diverges dramatically in how the costs of the system are divided between workers and employers. The parties shared the costs under the German system, but the employer exclusively finances the system in North America. This allocation is based on the theory that work injuries are a cost of production, so it was argued that the employer should finance the system. In this respect, the North American workers' compensation system reflects the influence of British "friendly societies," which were operated by collectives of workers to help workers who had become injured at work or otherwise. Typically, in exchange for a promise that the workers would not sue over workplace injuries, employers contributed to the friendly societies.

Within a particular jurisdiction, employers pay workers' compensation premiums based on their industry group. There can be variation in the rate paid by a particular employer within an industry group based on claims cost experience, premium discounts, or myriad other factors (see Thomason, Schmidle, and Burton, 2001). In jurisdictions in the United States, competitive pressures among workers' compensation insurance firms may also influence the assessment rate paid by an employer. In most jurisdictions, very large employers can self-insure, and small employers may be allowed to self-insure as a group.

Workers' compensation costs in both Canada and the United States increased rapidly from the 1970s to the 1990s, and it is largely this apparent "crisis" that provided the impetus for recent reforms. In the United States, workers' compensation costs increased from $4.9 billion in 1970 to $60.1 billion in 1993. Since 1993, costs have declined to $55.2 billion in 1996.[3] In Canada, between 1970 and 1992, workers' compensation costs increased from Can.$308 million to Can.$5.3 billion. Costs have since declined to Can.$4.9 billion in 1996.

WHO PAYS FOR WORKPLACE INJURIES?

With access to the courts largely preempted, there exist three mechanisms through which workers can receive compensation for the risk of injuries and illnesses that arise out of, or in the course of, employment: the market mechanism, collective bargaining, and legislation in the form of mandated workers' compensation.

Workers may be compensated for the risk of injury through the wage-setting process in the labor market. Holding all other factors constant, workers in relatively risky jobs will earn greater total wages and fringe benefits than otherwise similar workers who face a lower degree of risk. Fully efficient compensating wage differentials (i.e., differentials that fully compensate the worker for risk and result in socially optimal investments in safety) will arise if workers and firms are aware of workplace risks; product, labor, and other factor markets are perfectly competitive; there are no transactions costs associated with negotiating and enforcing contracts; there exists full experience rating of workers' compensation (or other related) insurance; individual workers value risk at the same rate as society as a whole; and workers are risk neutral and fully mobile.

Even if all of these assumptions do not hold in a particular setting, or hold only approximately, compensating differentials for risk may still arise from labor markets. Viscusi (1993) reviewed the vast empirical literature on compensating differentials for the risk of fatal and nonfatal injuries. In general, labor markets appear generally to give rise to compensating differentials for fatal and nonfatal risk (with some exceptions), but the magnitudes of the risk premiums reported vary substantially from study to study. Since theory gives no guidance on what the magnitude of the efficient compensating differential should be, there is no clear way of determining which of these studies is producing "correct" results. In addition, the literature is replete with criticisms of these studies, most of which consist of highlighting the likelihood that the real world varies in important ways from the theory that generates efficient differentials, as well as a plethora of data and statistical problems. Together, these factors led Ehrenberg (1988) to conclude that "the potential usefulness for public policy in occupational health and safety of estimates of compensating wage differentials for injury risk is limited."

Even where an efficient wage premium is paid that fully compensates workers for the <u>expected</u> costs of a workplace injury, the <u>actual</u> cost of a workplace injury that falls on the worker who is unfortunate enough to suffer one can be substantially greater than the accumulated compensating wages. This injured worker may then be faced with relying on social assistance or some other income support program if one is available. The distaste of society for thrusting workers who suffer injuries, and their families, into poverty was one of the early rationales for an *ex ante* work injury compensation scheme (Larson and Larson 1998: p. 1–5).

Collective bargaining provides another mechanism through which workers may be compensated for risk of workplace injuries (as well as having a potential role in injury prevention). Some empirical evidence (e.g., Viscusi 1980; Olson 1981; Dorsey 1983; Dorsey and Walzer 1983; and Fishback and Kantor 1995) suggests that unionized workers receive higher risk premiums than otherwise similar nonunion workers. In some instances, compensating differentials are formalized in the form of "danger pay" provisions for particular workers who face exposures to risk in excess of those faced by other members of the bargaining unit. Unions may also negotiate insurance benefits that supplement those paid through workers' compensation. In addition, unions can ensure that workers' rights to injury compensation are protected through the grievance process.

However, collective bargaining has its own set of limitations as a mechanism for allocating the costs of work injuries. First, fewer and fewer workers are covered by collective bargaining in the United States and, to a lesser extent, Canada, and far less than a plurality of workers are so covered in both countries. In addition, the existence of a union as a bargaining agent for workers does not ensure that the union will have sufficient bargaining power to secure benefits for work injuries, nor even that a bargained result will be superior to the market outcome.

The weaknesses of the market mechanism and collective bargaining are often cited as rationales for legislation that mandates workers' compensation coverage. As described earlier, workers' compensation is financed, in the first instance, by employers. While the initial incidence of the workers' compensation tax clearly falls on the employer, it is less clear where the ultimate incidence of the cost of the tax lies. The tax could be paid for by the consumers, in the form of higher prices for goods and services. The tax could be shifted to owners or shareholders of the firm in the form of lower profits, or it could be shifted to workers in the form of lower wages and benefits. The expectation that the shift to workers might occur was anticipated by one of the pioneers of workers' compensation in North America, Sir William

Meredith. In his 1913 report that laid the groundwork for the Ontario (Canada) workers' compensation legislation, he noted that

> The burden that the workman is required to bear (as a result of a workplace injury) he cannot shift upon the shoulders of anyone else, but the employer may and no doubt will shift this burden upon the shoulders of the community, or if he has any difficulty in doing that will by reducing the wages of his workmen compel them to bear part of it. (P. 15)

As Chelius and Burton (1994a) carefully described, the ultimate incidence of the workers' compensation tax depends critically on conditions in both labor and product markets. An increase in the cost of production associated with an increase in the workers' compensation tax will induce firms to produce less output. This will have the impact of increasing the price of the good, thereby reducing demand. The extent of the reduction in demand for the good will depend on just how sensitive the demand for the product is to changes in its price. If the demand for the product is price elastic, then small increases in the price will produce disproportionately large reductions in the demand. Similarly, if demand for the good is price inelastic, an increase in the price of the product will result in disproportionately small reductions in demand.

The labor and product markets are inextricably linked. Reductions in demand for the product implies that fewer workers will be required to produce goods, so firms will demand fewer workers and wages will fall. Over time, firms will also adjust their production processes to use fewer workers (who have become more expensive as a result of the workers' compensation tax) and more of other inputs, such as machines, in order to reduce costs. This will also result in a reduction in the demand for workers. Holding the labor supply choices of workers' constant, the more elastic the labor demand curve, the greater will be the reduction in the money wage.

Similarly, holding the elasticity of the labor demand curve constant, the more inelastic the supply of labor, the greater will be the reduction in the money wage paid to workers given a decrease in labor demand. For example, if the labor supply curve were perfectly inelastic (i.e., the supply of workers is invariant to the wage), a reduction in demand would cause the money wage would to fall to a level that fully offsets the cost of the tax. That is, the cost of the tax would be entirely shifted to workers in the form of reduced wages.

Establishing that the elasticities of demand and supply are important for determining the extent to which the costs of workers' compensation are shifted to workers is important because a number of factors can influence these elasticities and these factors can change over time. If one conjectures that costs are increasingly being shifted to workers, it must be established that labor demand has become more elastic over time and/or that labor supply has become more inelastic over time.

Economic theory suggests the conditions under which the labor demand curve can be expected to be relatively elastic. These conditions are commonly termed the Hicks-Marshall laws of derived demand. In particular, labor demand is likely to be relatively elastic when the demand for the product produced by the workers is relatively elastic, when it is technically and/or institutionally easy to substitute other inputs in the production process for labor, when the supply of substitute inputs in inelastic, and, generally, when labor costs are a relatively large component of the total costs of production.

It should also be noted that if workers actually value the workers' compensation component of their pay package—that is, they value workers' compensation insurance more than the cost equivalent paid in money wages—workers will increase their supply of labor at all wage rates and accept more of the cost of providing the benefit.

There has been considerable interest in determining the ultimate incidence of workers' compensation payroll taxes because understanding the true cost incidence of the tax permits policymakers to determine the extent to which changes in the costs of workers' compensation programs will influence the competitiveness of firms and the financial well-being of both injured and uninjured workers. Of particular interest to researchers are the issues of the existence and extent of the workers' compensation tax pass-back to workers and the mechanism through which workers' compensation, and more generally the risk of injury, affects wages. With respect to the latter issue, where *ex post* compensation for workplace injuries exists (as is the case with workers' compensation), *ex ante* compensation in the form of compensating wage differentials should be lower than would exist in the absence of employer-sponsored accident insurance.

There have been a number of studies examining the impact of workers' compensation benefits on wages and other fringe benefits. Of these studies, the more recent works by Viscusi and Moore (1987), Moore and Viscusi (1990), Gruber and Krueger (1991), and Fishback and Kantor (1995) are of particular significance because they address many of the important measurement and methodological problems arising in the earlier pioneering studies.[4]   Some Canadian evidence on this issue comes from Vaillancourt and Marceau (1990).

Viscusi and Moore (1987) estimated a model that included a workers' compensation benefit measure which varied across jurisdictions and across individuals within a given workers' compensation jurisdiction, according to whether the individual's benefit would be subject to statutorily defined minimum or maximum benefit levels. Viscusi and Moore also explicitly accounted for the favorable tax treatment of workers' compensation benefits. The generosity of workers' compensation benefits was measured by the proportion of earnings replaced by workers' compensation, after applying appropriate statistical procedures to address the endogeneity of the replacement rate and the wage rate.

They estimated a hedonic wage equation on the annual rate of lost workday injuries and illnesses as well as the annual rate of all injuries and illness (including those for which no workdays were lost), a binary measure indicating whether the worker reported the belief that their job exposed them to physical dangers or unhealthy conditions, and a number of other socioeconomic variables. The model was estimated on 485 nonfarm, non-self-employed, household heads that worked at least 20 hours per week. The sample was drawn from the 1977 Quality of Employment Survey, which contained information on 1976 work experience. In order to ensure that "wage differentials were not contaminated by hours effects" (p. 253), they estimated the model on hourly wages.

A number of equations were estimated on both the log and level of hourly wages. Viscusi and Moore argued that, since workers' compensation will affect wages only when the level of risk is greater than zero, the replacement rate should be interacted with the accident rate variables. In general, they found that the inclusion of the replacement rate on its own resulted in more precise parameter estimates on the risk variables, but it did not alter their magnitudes. However, when the replacement rate was entered interactively with the risk variables, the risk coefficients generally increased in magnitude. In this framework, the replacement rate/risk interaction variables were generally negative and significant, suggesting that the costs of workers' compensation are at least partially paid in the form of lower wages.

Gruber and Krueger (1991) motivated their investigation of the incidence of workers' compensation costs by citing the inconsistent results of the studies that have attempted to measure wage-fringe bene-fit trade-offs in general. They suggested that a potential cause of these confounding results may lie in the fact that many studies of mandated insurance rely on small degrees of interjurisdictional or intertemporal variation to identify a trade-off. They argued that any effect may be lost by omitted cross-state factors, offering union power as an example of such an omitted variable.

The authors estimated a panel model of wages, controlling for fixed jurisdictional (state) and time effects. To ensure high degrees of cross-sectional and intertemporal variation, they used data from five high-risk industries (truck driving, carpentry, plumbing, gas station attending, and nonprofessional hospital employment). The data were taken from the Current Population Surveys of 1979, 1980, 1981, 1987, and 1989. Their workers' compensation cost variable was the employer's assessment rate per $100 of payroll. They found a statisti-cally significant negative trade-off only in the case of the truck driver subsample. A negative trade-off in the pooled subsample was found only when state dummy variables and state dummies interacted with occupation dummies were included in the regression. They estimated that 86.5 percent of workers' compensation cost increases were passed on to workers in the form of lower wages. Using data from an employer survey, the authors also found a small but statistically insig-nificant negative employment effect associated with increased workers' compensation benefits.

In an important study, Fishback and Kantor (1995) used historical data from relatively dangerous industries (coal, lumber and building trades) from the early 1900s, during which time workers' compensa-tion statutes were being enacted in the United States, to examine the extent to which the costs of workers' compensation was ultimately passed back to workers wages. Their careful study revealed that, in general, workers paid for at least the costs of expected benefits from the workers' compensation system and, in some instances, even appear to have paid for the entire costs of providing the workers compensation insurance (i.e., the expected benefits plus all of the costs of providing coverage, such as administration, insurance industry profits, and so forth). They also found that workers in the heavily unionized building trades sector paid a lower share of the costs of workers' compensation than did workers who were not unionized.

Vaillancourt and Marceau (1990) showed evidence for Canada that the incidence of workers' compensation payroll taxes may be different than that of other types of payroll taxes. They argued that, when workers' compensation payroll taxes increase because an underlying condition at work has deteriorated (such as increased risk of injury or disease), then the tax increase may be coincident with a reduction in labor supply as relatively risk averse workers leave that particular labor market. As a result, the ultimate shifting of the tax is not as straightforward as would be the case when an increase in the payroll tax merely initiates a reduction in labor demand by firms. Their estimation results suggest that about 85 percent of workers' compensation payroll taxes are shifted back to wages.

Taken together, these studies demonstrate a negative relationship between wages and workers' compensation benefits. The reduction in wages per dollar of workers' compensation costs is somewhere between 50 cents and a dollar, with some consensus that about 80–85 percent of costs are passed back to workers.[5] Also, as Moore and Viscusi (1990, p.23) asserted, the studies to date have established that, "wage-risk differentials would be much higher in the absence of workers' compensation, as workers would demand more *ex ante* compensation for exposure to risk in the absence of *ex post* guarantees."

Thus, increases in the costs of workers' compensation associated with either increased risk of injury or disease, improved benefit generosity, or broader application of compensation to previously uncovered injuries or diseases are borne, to a large extent, by workers. It is conceivable that, to the extent that product markets have become more competitive (i.e., product demand curves and therefore labor demand curves have become more price elastic), the pressure to shift a greater amount of the costs of workplace injuries to workers is intensifying.

Wages, workers' compensation benefits, and risk of injury are all interrelated. Understanding the interrelations is essential for formulating policy designed at reducing the costs of workplace injuries. If reductions in the costs of injuries are due to reductions in one of the dimensions of generosity of workers' compensation, without any true reduction in the costs of injuries, then the likely outcome will be an increase in compensating wage differentials to cover the uninsured risk. Also, the costs of injuries to workers who are unable to obtain compensating wages will fall on to either other social safety nets (e.g., Social Security Disability Insurance [SSDI] or Canada Pension Plan [CPP] Disability Insurance in Canada) or workers and/or their families. In other words, there will be no "real resource savings"; rather, the costs will simply be transferred, and there will be costs associated with effecting the transfer (e.g., litigation).

On the other hand, if the reduction in costs of workers' compensation come as a result of true resource savings, as would be the case if there were improvements in health and safety practices which reduced the risk of injury, then compensating wage differentials would be reduced and the savings from workers' compensation costs would be split between workers and firms. Under this scenario, costs are genuinely reduced and not simply transferred.

THE CURRENT CLIMATE IN WORKERS' COMPENSATION

Workers' compensation legislation in the United States was founded on 11 basic principles (Association of Workers' Compensation Boards of Canada 1993): 1) workers' compensation is the exclusive remedy for workplace injuries; 2) employers fund the system so that the costs of workplace injuries are built into the costs of products and shared by all consumers of those products; 3) fault or negligence is excluded from consideration in determining benefit eligibility; 4) the philosophy of the system is social rather than legalistic, with efforts focused on assisting injured workers; 5) benefits are paid for disability only and not pain and suffering; 6) compensation is to be adequate to ensure the worker will not become a burden to others; 7) benefits cease upon the death of the worker, unless the worker's death was attributable to the work injury; 8) benefits are to be paid through a system guided by insurance principles; 9) some workers are exempt from coverage, where such coverage was impractical; 10) premiums are experience rated; and 11) state agencies, government departments, and courts monitor the system and resolve disputes.

Driven by pressures to control the escalating costs of workers' compensation, there has been a significant withdrawal from the traditional notions of the collective protection of workers from the costs associated with workplace injuries. Thomason, Schmidle, and Burton (2001) have calculated comprehensive indices of the generosity of workers' compensation indemnity benefits for the United States. They found that the generosity of most types of benefits had been increasing until about 1991. However, since that time, a downward trend appears to be emerging in the generosity of temporary total disability benefits and permanent partial disability benefits for relatively minor disabilities. Since these together account for a significant portion of benefit costs, the relative generosity of the workers' compensation system as a whole appears to be declining.

However, reduced benefit generosity is only one mechanism through which the costs of workplace risk can be shifted more directly to workers. Benefit generosity is a function of both the actual dollar value of the benefits and the probability that the injury or illness suffered by the worker will ultimately be compensated. A doubling of the dollar value of benefits may appear to be a considerable increase in generosity but, if the probability of the benefit is reduced, then the expected value of the benefit is also reduced. What might reduce the probability of a claim being accepted?

Many of these factors relate to the definition of a compensable injury. Once there is evidence that the accident actually occurred and that the condition(s) from which the worker is suffering can reasonably be attributed to the injury or illness, workers' compensation authorities must determine the answer to the following three questions in order to deem a particular injury or accident compensable: 1) is there an "employer" as defined by the statute, 2) is the worker making the claim a "worker" as defined by the legislation, and 3) did the personal injury arise out of and in the course of employment? The answer to the first question addresses whether the employer is covered by workers' compensation legislation, perhaps for any of the reasons outlined earlier, or if the worker is self-employed and had elected not to purchase workers' compensation insurance. The second question establishes whether the worker had an employment relationship with the employer that entailed workers' compensation coverage. The third question represents a three-part test: the personal injury suffered by the worker has to be an injury or illness covered by the legislation, the injury arises out of employment if the worker was properly performing assigned tasks when the injury occurred, and the injury occurs in the course of employment when it happens on the employers premises during working hours.

Recent workers' compensation reform efforts across North America have contained elements which effectively "redefine" a compensable injury or illness in the following forms:

1) The exclusion of certain types of claims from compensation, such as chronic stress or repetitive strain injuries.

2) Removal of coverage under the legislation—some workers are not covered and others may be increasingly not covered because they are encouraged by employers to become independent contractors or piece workers in response to high workers' compensation costs.

3) Reduction in the amount of time after an injury occurs during which a worker can file a claim. For some injuries and many illnesses there can be a considerable latency period between the time of the accident and when the disorder is manifest.

Because of the multitude of workers' compensation jurisdictions in North America, and the fact that workers' compensation legislation is frequently amended, it is not practical to enumerate all of the reform efforts. However, it is possible to provide some specific examples from Canada and the United States to demonstrate a more general trend:[6]

- The Province of Ontario introduced legislation that will reduce benefits from 90 percent of net earnings to 85 percent; indexation of benefits will be reduced from the current factor of 100 percent to less than 75 percent of the inflation rate and capped at a maximum annual adjustment of 4 percent, except for the permanently disabled and survivors of deceased workers; entitlement to benefits for stress and repetitive strain injuries will be restricted; and workers will be required to apply for benefits within six months of the date of injury (previously, they could apply at any time).

- Amendments to the Nova Scotia Workers' Compensation Act in 1995 and 1996 included a deductible of two-fifths of the workers' net weekly compensation rate (in effect, a two-day waiting period) for injuries requiring absences from work of less than five weeks; a reduction in the benefit rate for temporary disabilities from 75 percent of gross earnings to 75 percent of net earnings for the first 26 weeks of absence from work, increasing to 85 percent thereafter; integration of employer supplementary benefits with workers' compensation benefits, such that the total of all benefits does not exceed 85 percent of preinjury net earnings (previously 100 percent); and the exclusion of stress as a compensable injury.

- In 1993, Connecticut reduced total and partial disability benefits, as well as fatality benefits, from 80 percent to 75 percent of the worker's average weekly wage after federal and state taxes, and reduced the maximum weekly compensation benefit from 150 percent to 100 percent of the state's average weekly wage.

- The Massachusetts reforms of 1991 reduced benefits to 60 percent of gross wages from 66.6 percent, and substantially reduced the maximum period over which injured workers could collect benefits.

- Effective January 1, 1993, Maine reduced maximum weekly benefits to the higher of $441 or 90 percent of the state average weekly wage, reduced the maximum duration of compensation for minor permanent disabilities from 500 weeks to 260 weeks (while reclassifying many permanent disabilities as minor), and removed inflation adjustment on permanent partial disability and death benefits, among other changes.

- Oregon introduced reforms in 1987 and 1990 that made stricter the definition of compensable injuries and diseases, limited the use of vocational rehabilitation services, limited access to appeals of claims decisions, and limited physician choice and use of particular types of medical rehabilitation services.

- Washington State, in 1985, repealed mandatory vocational rehabilitation and gave employers the option of deducting up to 20 percent of the cost of workers' compensation premiums from employee paychecks.

One possible metric of the effects of workers' compensation reforms is their impact on the proportion of claims that are ultimately determined to be compensable. Following the Oregon reforms, claim denial rates increased from 12.9 percent in 1988 to 28.5 percent in 1991. In Canada, the proportion of claims that ultimately were not compensated, either due to denials or workers abandoning their claims, stood at 4.7 percent in 1973. By 1993, this proportion had increased to 15.6 percent.

Of course, this trend represents real improvement to the extent that the increasing numbers of claims denials and abandonments is due to better administration or detection of fraud. However, to the extent that increased denials and abandonments reflect a move to simply redefining previously costly and difficult-to-adjudicate claims as noncompensable, they represent a tangible measure of shifting the costs of injuries more directly on to individual injured workers.

It is reasonable to suggest that reductions in benefit levels and "redefinitions" of what constitutes a compensable injury are likely to disproportionately affect the contingent workforce. There is evidence that contingent workers are more likely to suffer injuries than are workers in more traditional employment relationships. In noting that temporary workers, business service employment, and production subcontracting accounted for a large (10 percent in 1986) and growing proportion of employment relationships, Rebitzer (1995) examined the extent to which contract employees receive adequate safety training and supervision in the context of the U.S. petrochemical industry. He found that incentives created by the accident liability system encouraged petrochemical plant management to divest responsibility for training and supervision to managers of the subcontracting firm and that this training and supervision is likely to be inferior to that offered by the host company. His empirical investigation suggests that, other factors constant, workers of subcontractors are more likely to experience accidents than workers hired directly by the firm, heightened supervision by the host firm could reduce the accident rates of contract workers (but is unlikely because such supervision could have accident liability consequences for the host firm), and safety training received by contract workers is less effective in improving safety than that received by workers hired directly by the host firm.

Hebdon and Hyatt (1997) showed evidence that unionized part-time workers in Ontario are significantly less likely to pursue formal occupational health and safety complaints or to refuse unsafe work than are otherwise similar full-time workers. To the extent that this reveals some reluctance among part-time workers to exercise their legislated rights to protect themselves from unsafe work environments, these contingent workers may be exposed to greater risks than their full-time counterparts.

The growing use of contingent workers and the increased likelihood of injuries associated with contingent work are being met with a decrease in the likelihood that the injury will be compensated and reductions in benefits for those injuries that are compensated.

Some reforms could conceivably result in certain contingent workers being ineligible for benefits all together. For example, employers may require that workers essentially become self-employed and contract with the employer to provide services. Even though the nature of the employment relationship would have undergone only a cosmetic change, the employer could be absolved of liability for injuries. Workers who take work into their own homes, or who "telecommute," may find that they are ineligible for compensation since their injury did not occur on the employer's premises.

There is also evidence that downsizing may increase the number of accidents. Anderson and Buchholz (1988) found that accident frequency in both the durable goods and nondurable goods manufacturing sectors in the United States increased with the use of overtime and with turnover rates. A recent study by the American Management Association and Cigna (reported in the *Wall Street Journal* [Jeffrey 1996]) found a greater increase in disability claims rates among companies that downsized since 1990 than for firms that did not downsize. To the extent that access to and levels of workers' compensation benefits are being reduced, workers may experience the burden of increased disability costs in addition to the dislocation costs of economic restructuring.

Changes in the nature and content of work expose workers to different risks than was the case when the workers' compensation system was conceived. Traumatic injuries (broken bones and contusions) where there is a direct causal link between the event that caused the injury and the consequences of the injury, common in manufacturing settings, are becoming proportionately less frequent. More common are repetitive strain injuries, such as those commonly associated with computer keyboards, which do not have an immediate onset and may also be influenced or aggravated by nonworkplace factors. The absence of a direct causal link between work and the injury reduces the likelihood that the worker will receive compensation for these types of injuries.

It should be noted that, in addition to changes in workers' compensation legislation, changes in the administration of workers' compensation statutes by insurance companies or workers' compensation authorities can also have the impact of shifting risk back to workers. For example, increases in appeals and delays in processing workers' compensation claims experienced in both the United States and Canada may be evidence of employers' tenacity to reduce costs. It has been suggested that employers have responded to increasing costs by trying to suppress claims by encouraging workers not to report but paying them their salaries or by intimidation and other such strategies. However, the evidence in this area is anecdotal at best. One way that nonreporting pressures on injured workers can show up is through workers' interactions with their (usually) family physicians treating the injuries. Based on a recent survey, the Ontario Medical Association reported that 65 percent of its member physicians had been asked by workers not to report an office visit as being work injury related (the cost of which would be billed to the workers' compensation board and would also have the effect of notifying the workers' compensation authority that an accident had occurred).

In general then, the foci of the reforms have been to tighten entitlement to workers' compensation benefits by precluding certain conditions from coverage or otherwise changing the definition of what constituted a compensable injury or illness, reducing benefit levels (particularly in Canadian jurisdictions), and creating (financial) incentives to reduce the duration on disability benefits and hasten the return to work. These sorts of changes to the workers' compensation system have not been consistent with the changing nature of work and the workplace, and they more directly shift the costs of injuries onto workers.

Burton (1996, p. 5) summarized the recent trends in workers' compensation as follows:

> ". . . as the 1990s have progressed, the statutory protection and actual benefits paid to workers have deteriorated, while the costs for employers have stabilized and the profits for workers' compensation insurers have soared."

It is critical to make two points. First, it does not necessarily follow that because the reforms effectively reduce benefits available to workers, such reforms are always inappropriate. In some instances, there is little evidence that services provided through the workers' compensation system have significant impact on worker well-being—vocational rehabilitation being a (controversial) example. It may also be the case that system utilization was higher than optimal, although the usual metric of this that underlies reform effort is escalating system costs. What has been absent is any convincing evidence of substantial fraud or evidence that workers were being "over-compensated." Second, many of the workers' compensation reform packages in North America have also included components that focus on improving injury prevention and enhanced return-to-work initiatives and incentives. To the extent that these efforts are successful, there is the potential for true resource savings and not simply transfer savings.

WORKERS' COMPENSATION REFORM BACKLASH

The workers' compensation system does not exist in a vacuum. Indeed, the system can be characterized as a balloon—pressure in one spot will cause a compensating "bulge" in another. Public policies to reduce costs to the workers' compensation that do not manifest in real reductions in the frequency and severity of injuries, but rather just reductions in benefit generosity, will have consequences, some of which are beginning to be revealed. Important among these is a breakdown of the historic compromise and a return to tort litigation.

A spate of recent court cases in the United States suggests that where an injury or illness is not covered by workers' compensation legislation, workers may be relieved from the exclusivity of the workers' compensation remedy and be given leave to sue their employers. The basic issue that the courts have been asked to decide is what the exclusivity provision of workers' compensation legislation covers. For example, it is clear that workers not covered by workers' compensation legislation can sue their employers in the event of a workplace injury or illness, but can workers who are covered by the legislation sue their employer if a particular injury or illness is not covered by the legislation? In two important U.S. cases, courts have found that workers can sue under these circumstances.

In *Errand v. Cascade Steel Rolling Mills* (888 P.2d 544 Oregon 1995), the Supreme Court of Oregon reversed a court of appeals decision denying Errand the right to sue his employer for an irritation of the upper respiratory tract as a result of exposure to chemicals in the workplace. The court held that, since Errand's injury was deemed not compensable under Oregon's Workers' Compensation Law, he could bring a civil action against the employer. Originally, the Court of Appeals had held that, "The exclusivity of the Act is not limited to claims that are ultimately determined to be compensable" (*Errand v. Cascade Steel Rolling Mills, Inc*, 126 Or.App. at 453-54, 869 P.2d 358). Before the Supreme Court of Oregon, counsel for Errand argued that since his claim for workers' compensation was denied on the grounds that he had a pre-existing condition and that exposure to chemicals in the workplace was not the "major cause" of his condition, his condition was not subject to the exclusivity of remedy provision.

The court's decision appeared to hinge on whether the exclusivity provisions of the law should be invoked for only those injuries and diseases that are compensable under the law, or whether it should be invoked more broadly as covering all work-related injuries or diseases, whether or not there is sufficient evidence to establish that the worker is entitled to compensation for the injury. The majority of the *Errand* court held that "the exclusivity provision of . . . (the Oregon workers' compensation law) . . . does not provide defendant with immunity to civil claims here, because plaintiff did not have a 'compensable' injury within the meaning of . . . (the Oregon workers' compensation law)."

In *Stratemeyer v. Lincoln County* (915 P.2d 175 Montana 1996), a Montana Sheriff's officer sought leave to sue his employer after his workers' compensation claim for mental injuries suffered upon witnessing the final stages of a suicide was denied on the basis that such injuries were not covered by the Montana Workers' Compensation Act. What was particularly important about this case was that the relevant legislation invoked the exclusivity of the workers' compensation remedy, "for all *employments* covered by the Act . . ." as opposed to injuries covered under the Act, as was the case in Errand. The majority of the Court stated that, "The *quid pro quo* between employers and employees is central to the Act; thus, it is axiomatic that there must be some possibility of recovery by the employee for the compromise to hold." (p. 179) The majority concluded that

> it is unequivocally clear that mental injuries, such as Stratemeyer's, are beyond the scope of coverage of the Workers' Compensation Act.   Accordingly, under Lincoln County's theory, employees would have no possibility of recovery for mental injuries and yet the employer would be shielded from all potential liability.   If that were the case, the quid pro quo, which is the foundation of the exclusive remedy rule would be eliminated. Such a result would be contrary to the spirit and intent of the Workers' Compensation Act.

The court gave Stratemeyer leave to proceed with a tort claim against Lincoln County.

In Canada, some workers' compensation activists have considered the possibility to mounting a constitutional challenge to the exclusive remedy provisions of workers' compensation, in light of what they view as serious reductions in benefits. At issue is the interpretation of section 15 (1) of the Canadian Charter of Rights and Freedoms, which states, "Every individual is equal before and under the law and has the right to equal benefit of the law without discrimination . . ."

In an important and influential opinion, the Newfoundland Court of Appeal wrestled with the question of whether the exclusivity provision of the workers' compensation statute violated the s.15 protection against discrimination. Section 15, in other situations, had been applied to ensure that otherwise similar persons or groups be similarly treated. The question facing the court was whether exclusivity was discriminatory because some workers would receive lower benefits under workers' compensation than they would from a common law court. The court decided that the statute was not invalidated by this possibility. What is important is how the court came to this decision. Essentially, the court compared the "global advantages" of the statute to the tort actions which the statute precluded. The court noted that, among a number positive aspects, the workers' compensation legislation provided for good medical, lost wage, death, and other benefits, which were paid immediately and not subject to the solvency of the employer. The court also found that awards from common law courts may be superior in some ways, such as increased compensation for non-economic losses, but on balance, workers' compensation was found to be reasonable and fair, and the exclusivity principle was not unconstitutional. In 1989, the Supreme Court of Canada upheld this decision.

However, the court may have left open the possibility that any diminution of protection provided under the workers' compensation system relative to the common law tort system, could change the court's mind about the fairness of the exclusivity provisions of workers' compensation legislation. Continued diminution of workers' compensation benefits may invoke further constitutional challenges in Canada on these grounds.

Of course, the reintroduction of tort liability in the workers' compensation system carries with it great many disadvantages. The uncertainty and delay in the determination of liability and awards, which were features of the era before workers' compensation, are likely to resurface. To the extent that workers' compensation programs operate concurrently with tort liability for work-related injuries and illness, it is reasonable to expect that workers' compensation benefits, other fringe benefits, or wages will also be reduced in response to the increased costs of employment introduced by the return to tort. In addition, the parties may play the workers' compensation system and the tort system against each other as leverage to either securing an award or reducing the size of an award. For example, workers may file both a workers' compensation claim and a tort suit in the hope that the tort suit will pre-empt employer opposition to a workers' compensation claim (even though opposition to the claim may be warranted). On the other side of the coin, employers might introduce delay into the workers' compensation claims adjudication process, through a series of appeals, in order to induce workers into accepting a smaller tort award.

As described earlier, there has been an increase in the proportion of workers' compensation claims that have either been denied or abandoned. It would be useful to know whether workers whose claims were denied ultimately sought and received assistance from other social support programs, such as public disability pensions or social assistance. Unfortunately, few sources of data can address this question directly. Nonetheless, the reduction in the proportion of ultimately accepted workers' compensation claims roughly coincides with a doubling in the cost of Canada Pension Plan (CPP) disability pension expenditures (the Canadian equivalent to SSDI in the United States) over the period 1987–1994. Further, the Chief Actuary for Canada notes in the *Fifteenth Actuarial Report on the Canada Pension Plan* (1995, p. 58), ". . . musculoskeletal and mental cases have been subject to somewhat higher than average increases." While this information does not prove any causal relationship, it does suggest that a more careful examination of these trends is warranted.

Finally, the costs of accidents must be fully reflected in the price of the good to ensure that the social optimal price reflects the danger to workers of producing the good. An important efficiency problem arises when the "correct" cost of accidents is not assessed to the employer—experience-rating incentives to improve safety are diminished, product prices are suboptimally low, profits are inefficiently high, and workers are exposed to inefficiently high levels of risk.

CONCLUDING REMARKS

Escalating costs in the workers' compensation programs across North America has engendered significant policy responses. While the theory and evidence summarized in the third section of this chapter demonstrated that workers have traditionally borne the costs of workers' compensation through smaller pay packets, this indirect method of cost shifting may take time to effect. Many of the recent workers' compensation legislative reforms have been "redistributive" in nature, largely in the direction of individual workers assuming a greater direct burden of the costs of workplace injuries and illnesses.

Reforms to the workers' compensation system do not occur in a vacuum. Delisting coverage of particular injuries or illnesses may result in a return to tort remedies and undermine the historic compromise of workers' compensation. In addition, to the extent that the workers' compensation system successfully reduces costs by lowering benefits and removing coverage, these costs are likely to be transferred to other social programs, other forms of private insurance, and on to injured workers and their families.

Certainly efficiency problems are created when the costs of injuries and illness are misassigned. A coordinated effort among administrators of government programs, insurers, workers, and employers to effect the correct allocation of costs is an essential, but practically difficult, endeavour. Most importantly, the surest way to reduce the real resource costs of workplace injuries and illness is through initiatives that reduce their incidence.

Notes

1. For an excellent review of permanent disability compensation schemes under workers' compensation, see Berkowitz and Burton (1987).
2. The discontinuity in the lost-time series for the United States is the result of a methodological change by the Social Security Administration, which collects and reports these data.
3. For an informative discussion regarding trends in workers' compensation costs and benefits in the United States, see Spieler and Burton (1998).
4. Some of the earlier studies include Arnould and Nichols (1983), Dorsey (1983), Dorsey and Walzer (1983), Butler (1983), and Ruser (1985). For a more complete review of this literature, see Chelius and Burton (1994b).
5. There is some evidence that unionized workers appear to have not experienced the same degree of cost shifting as nonunion workers (see, in particular, Dorsey and Walzer 1983 and Fishback and Kantor 1995).
6. It should be noted that many of the legislative reforms cited below were also accompanied by some improvements, such as increases in earnings ceilings, limited reemployment rights, and other changes. However, since the general purpose of many reforms is to address a perceived financial crisis, it is assumed that changes bringing about reductions in pay-outs are of paramount importance in the total reform packages.

References

Anderson, Evan E., and Rogene A. Buchholz. 1988. "Economic Instability and Occupational Injuries: The Impact of Overtime Hours and Turnover Rates." *Labor Studies Journal* 14(Winter): 33–49.

Arnould, Richard J., and Len M. Nichols. 1983. "Wage-Risk Premiums and Workers' Compensation: A refinement of Estimates of Compensating Wage Differentials." *Journal of Political Economy* 91(2): 332–340.

Association of Workers' Compensation Boards of Canada. 1993. *Comparison of Canadian and United States Workers' Compensation Systems.* Edmonton: AWCBC.

Berkowitz, Monroe, and John F. Burton, Jr. 1987. *Permanent Disability Benefits in Workers' Compensation.* Kalamazoo, Michigan: W.E. Upjohn Institute for Employment Research.

Burton, John F., Jr. 1996. "Workers' Compensation Benefits, Costs and Profits: An Overview of Developments in the 1990's." *Workers' Compensation Monitor* 9(November/December): 1–5, 12.

Burton, John F., Jr., and Timothy P. Schmidle, eds. 1996. *1996 Workers' Compensation Year Book.* Horsham, Pennsylvania: LRP Publications.

Butler, Richard J. 1983. "Wage and Injury Rate Response to Shifting Levels of Workers' Compensation." In *Safety and the Workforce*, John D. Worrall, ed. Ithaca, New York: ILR Press.

Chelius, James R., and John F. Burton, Jr. 1994a. "Who Actually Pays for Workers' Compensation? Theory." In *1995 Workers' Compensation Year Book*, John F. Burton, Jr. and Timothy P. Schmidle, eds. Horsham, Pennsylvania: LRP Publications.

_____. 1994b. "Who Actually Pays for Workers' Compensation? The Empirical Evidence." In *1995 Workers' Compensation Year Book*, John F. Burton, Jr. and Timothy P. Schmidle, eds. Horsham, Pennsylvania: LRP Publications.

Dorsey, Stuart. 1983. "Employment Hazards and Fringe Benefits: Further Tests for Compensation Differentials." In *Safety and the Workforce*, John D. Worrall, ed. Ithaca, New York: ILR Press.

Dorsey, Stuart, and Norman Walzer. 1983. "Workers' Compensation, Job Hazards, and Wages." *Industrial and Labor Relations Review* 36(July): 642–654.

Ehrenberg, Ronald G. 1988. "Workers' Compensation, Wages, and the Risk of Injury." In *New Perspectives in Workers' Compensation*, John F. Burton, Jr., ed. Ithaca, New York: ILR Press.

Fishback, Price V., and Shawn Everett Kantor. 1995. "Did Workers Pay for the Passage of Workers' Compensation Laws?" *Quarterly Journal of Economics* 110(August): 713–742.

Gruber, Jonathan, and Alan B. Krueger. 1991. "The Incidence of Mandated Employer-Provided Insurance: Lessons from Workers' Compensation Insurance." In *Tax Policy and the Economy*, D. Bradford, ed. Cambridge: Massachusetts: MIT Press.

Hebdon, Robert, and Douglas Hyatt. 1997. *The Impact of Industrial Relations (and Other Factors) on Health and Safety Conflict under the Internal Responsibility System.* Toronto: Centre for Industrial Relations, University of Toronto.

Human Resources Development Canada. 1997. "Table 250: Workers' Compensation, Total Payments, by Province and for Canada, Calendar Years 1970 to 1994." http://www.hrdc-drhc.gc.ca/hrdc/corp/stratpol/socpol/stats/tab250e.html.

Jeffrey, Nancy Ann. 1996. "Disability Claims Mirror Rising Job Cuts." *Wall Street Journal*, November 21: A2.

Larson, Arthur, and Lex K. Larson. 1998. *Larson's Workers' Compensation.* New York: Matthew Bender.

Meredith, Sir William Ralph. 1913. *Final Report on Laws Relating to the Liability of Employers to Make Compensation to Their Employees for Injuries Received in the Course of Their Employment which are in Force in other Countries.* Toronto: Queen's Printer.

Mont, Daniel, John F. Burton, Jr., and Virginia Reno. 1999. *Workers' Compensation: Benefits, Coverage, and Costs, 1996. New Estimates.* Washington, D.C.: National Academy of Social Insurance.

Moore, Michael J., and W. Kip Viscusi. 1990. *Compensating Mechanisms for Job Risks.* Princeton, New Jersey: Princeton University Press.

Olson, Craig A. 1981. "An Analysis of Wage Differentials Received by Workers on Dangerous Jobs." *Journal of Human Resources* 16(2): 408–416.

Rebitzer, James B. 1995. "Job Safety and Contract Workers in the Petrochemical Industry." *Industrial Relations* 34(January): 40–57.

Ruser, John W. 1985. "Workers' Compensation Benefits and Compensating Wage Differentials." Working paper 153, U.S. Bureau of Labor Statistics, Washington, D.C.

Spieler, Emily A. 1994. "Perpetuating Risk? Workers' Compensation and the Persistence of Occupational Injuries." *Houston Law Review* 31(1): 119–264.

Spieler, Emily A., and John F. Burton, Jr. 1998. "Compensation for Disabled Workers: Workers' Compensation." In *New Approaches to Disability in the Workplace*, Terry Thomason, John F. Burton, Jr., and Douglas Hyatt, eds. Ithaca, New York: Cornell University Press for the Industrial Relations Research Association.

Thomason, Terry, Timothy P. Schmidle, and John F. Burton, Jr. 2001. *Workers' Compensation: Benefits, Costs, and Safety under Alternative Insurance Arrangements.* Kalamazoo, Michigan: W.E. Upjohn Institute for Employment Research.

United States Chamber of Commerce. Various years. *Analysis of Workers' Compensation Laws of the United States.* Washington D.C.: The Chamber.

United States Department of Labor. 1996. *State Workers' Compensation Administrative Profiles.* Washington, D.C.: U.S. Department of Labor.

_____. 1997. *State Workers' Compensation Laws.* Washington, D.C.: U.S. Department of Labor.

Vaillancourt, Francois, and N. Marceau. 1990. "Do General and Firm-Specific Employer Payroll Taxes Have the Same Incidence? Theory and Evidence." *Economics Letters* 34: 175–181.

Viscusi, W. Kip. 1980. "Unions, Labor Market Structure, and Welfare Implications of the Quality of Work." *Journal of Labor Research* 1(Spring): 175–192.

_____. 1993. "The Value of Risks to Life and Health." *Journal of Economic Literature* 31(December): 1912–1946.

Viscusi, W. Kip, and Michael J. Moore. 1987. "Workers' Compensation: Wage Effects, Benefit Inadequacies, and the Value of Health Losses." *Review of Economics and Statistics* 69: 249–261.

The Authors

Robert B. Friedland is the founding Director of the Center on an Aging Society. The Center, which is a part of Georgetown University's Institute for Health Care Research and Policy, is a nonpartisan public policy institute that examines the issues that affect younger and older families and, in particular, the impact of changing demographics on employment, income, health, and long-term care.

Douglas E. Hyatt is an associate professor at the Centre for Industrial Relations, Rotman School of Management, and Scarborough College, all of which are at the University of Toronto. He is also a research associate of the Institute for Policy Analysis at the University of Toronto.

Sophie M. Korczyk is a consultant specializing in economic, statistical, and legislative analysis of social insurance programs; employee compensation and benefits; and government budget policies in the United States and overseas.

James E. Pesando received his B.A. from Harvard, his M.A. from the University of California at Berkeley, and his Ph.D. from the University of Toronto. He is currently a professor of economics at the University of Toronto and has published and consulted extensively in the area of public and private pensions.

Laura Summer is the deputy director for the Center on an Aging Society located at Georgetown University's Institute for Health Care Research and Policy.

John A. Turner works in the Public Policy Institute of AARP. He has a Ph.D. in economics from the University of Chicago and has nearly 100 publications focusing primarily on social security and pension issues.

Author Index

The italic letters *f*, *n*, or *t* following a page number indicate that the cited name is within a figure, note, or table, respectively, on that page.

Abraham, Katherine G., 7, 8, 17
Addison, John T., 39, 42, 47
AFL-CIO, 100, 113
Alpert, William T., 141, 157
Altonji, Joseph J., 20, 47
American Federation of Labor (AFL), 100, 113
Anderson, Evan E., 180, 187
Andolfatto, D., 23, 47
Arnould, Richard J., 187*n*4, 188
Association of Workers' Compensation Boards of Canada (AWCBC), 163, 175, 188
Auditor General of Canada, 108, 110, 113

Bagby, Nancy, 97, 99, 114
Baker, Michael, 22, 47
Baldwin, John, 21, 38, 47
Baumol, William J., 34, 43, 47
Belous, Richard S., 54, 56, 57, 80
Bennefield, Robert L., 88, 113
Bergman, Michael, 23–24, 47
Berkowitz, Monroe, 187*n*1, 188
Bernhardt, Annette, 29, 47
Bettinger, Douglas R., 156*n*7, 159
Black, Fischer, 152, 157
Blackburn, McKinley L., 39, 47
Bordo, Michael D., 23–24, 47
Borsjoly, Johanne, 33, 47
Braden, Bradley R., 85, 86, 114
Bregger, John E., 12, 17, 61, 80
Buchholz, Rogene A., 180, 187
Burkhauser, Richard V., 143, 157
Burton, John F., Jr., 163, 164, 167, 170, 176, 182, 187, 187*n*1, 187*n*3, 188, 189
Butler, Richard J., 187*n*4, 188

Calgary Herald, 19, 48
Carrington, William J., 36, 48
Chelius, James R., 170, 187, 188
Clark, Robert, 150, 157
Clinton, Angela, 62, 80
Cohany, Sharon R., 61, 63, 80
Commission for Labor Cooperation, 40, 41, 48, 78*n*2, 80
Commonwealth Fund, The, 93, 101, 114
Congress of Industrial Organizations (CIO), 100, 113
Corak, Miles, 22, 48
Cordes, Joseph J., 33, 36, 49
Cousineau, Jean-Michel, 38, 48

Dailey, Lorna M., 140, 148, 157
Davis, Karen, 94, 114
Davis, Steven J., 37, 41, 42, 48
den Broeder, Corina, 39, 47–48
Diebold, Francis X., 29, 48
Doescher, Tabitha A., 79*n*6, 80
Dorsey, Stuart, 169(2), 187*n*4, 187*n*5, 188
Drache, Daniel, 111, 113
Duca, John V., 42, 48
Duncan, Gregg J., 33, 47
Dunne, Timothy, 24, 38, 47, 48
duRivage, Virginia, 74, 76, 80

Eberts, Randall W., 9, 17
Ehrenberg, Ronald G., 168, 188
Employee Benefit Research Institute, 27, 48, 84, 87, 88, 90, 91, 92, 95, 98, 113
Evans, Robert, 111, 113–114
Executive Office of the President, 88, 114

Farber, Henry, 28, 29, 32, 34, 36, 48
Feldstein, Martin, 9, 17

Morissette, R., 43, 50
Morris, Martina, 29, 47
Murnane, Richard J., 24, 50
Murphy, Brian B., 132, 159

National Accounts Team, 85, 86, 114
Naylor, David C., 111, 114
Neumark, David, 28, 29, 48, 50
Nichols, Len M., 187n4, 188
North American Agreement on Labor
  Cooperation, 78n2, 80

Olson, Craig A., 169, 189
Organisation for Economic Co-operation
  and Development (OECD), 39, 50

Pattison, David, 145, 158
Payne, Jennifer, 133, 158
Pesando, James E., 2, 17, 122, 124, 125,
  129, 157n12, 158
Polivka, Anne, 53, 72, 73, 74, 75, 80
Polsky, D., 32–33, 36, 50
Polsky, Daniel, 28, 50
Polsky, David, 29, 48
Price Waterhouse LLP, 99, 114
Puleo, Elaine, 94, 114

Rafiquzzaman, M., 21, 47
Reagan, Patricia B., 143, 144, 158
Rebitzer, James B., 179, 189
Regenstein, Marsha, 97, 99, 114
Reno, Virginia, 163, 164, 189
Riddell, W. Craig, 21–22, 49
Roberts, Mark J., 24, 48
Rose, Stephen, 28, 29, 50
Rowland, Diane, 86, 94, 114
Ruhm, Christopher J., 42, 47
Ruser, John W., 187n4, 189

Saltford, Nancy, 58, 61, 72, 80
Samuelson, Larry, 24, 48
Schmidle, Timothy P., 167, 176, 188,
  189
Schmidt, Stefanie R., 19, 26, 28, 50

Schoen, Cathy, 94, 114
Schuh, Scott, 37, 41, 42, 48
Scott, Marc, 29, 47
Shoven, John B., 141, 157
Silow-Carroll, Andrew, 97, 99, 114
Smeeding, Timothy, 33, 47
Snider, Sarah, 58, 61, 72, 80
Solon, Gary, 22, 47
Spieler, Emily A., 163, 187n3, 189
Statistics Canada, 72, 80, 134, 156n9,
  158
Steinmeier, Thomas L., 150, 158
Stevens, Ann Huff, 27, 49
Stewart, Jay, 29, 50, 65, 80
Stone, Joe A., 9, 17
Sullivan, Daniel G., 30, 49
Sullivan, Terry, 111, 113
Svorny, Shirley V., 26, 28, 50
Swinnerton, Kenneth, 28, 29, 51

Tamagno, Edward, 119, 122, 129
Tepper, Irwin, 152, 158
Thomason, Terry, 167, 176, 189
Thompson, Mark, 2, 17, 44, 51
Topel, Robert, 6, 9, 17
Turner, John A., 37, 51, 140, 143, 144,
  148, 151, 157, 158

U.S. Bureau of the Census, 84, 87, 97,
  114(2)
U.S. Chamber of Commerce, 138, 158,
  163, 190
U.S. Department of Health and Human
  Services, 84, 85, 86, 87, 88, 89, 90,
  91, 92, 93, 94, 101, 114
U.S. Department of Labor, 26, 28, 30,
  34, 51, 54, 55, 56, 58, 60, 61, 62, 72,
  75, 79n3, 81, 136, 138, 141, 149,
  158, 163, 190
U.S. General Accounting Office, 137,
  158
Ureta, Manuelita, 28, 51

Vaillancourt, Francois, 172, 174, 190

Subject Index

The italic letters *f, n,* or *t* following a page number indicate that the subject information is within a figure, note, or table, respectively, on that page.

Defined benefit pensions (cont.)
  maximum benefit limits from, 148,
    151
  risks and, 116–118, 137, 150–153
  Registered Pension Plan and bridging
    supplement, 153–154
  taxes on, 152–153
Defined contribution pensions, 116–117,
    149
  cash balance plans with, features,
    137–138
  increase in, 132, 135, 141, 149, 155
  401(k) plans for, 137
  maximum contribution limits to,
    148–149, 151
  risks and, 116–118, 137–138,
    149–152
  taxes on, 151–153
DI. *See* Social Security Disability
    Insurance
Disability benefits, 79n5, 86, 180
  Canada Pension Plan and, 119, 175,
    186
  reduction of, 176–178, 181–182
  Social Security and, 63, 64, 85, 119,
    123, 175
  workers' compensation and,
    164–165, 175
Discrimination, 35, 184–185
Dislocated Workers Supplements, 32
Displaced Worker Survey, 31t, 35–36
Divorce, risk tolerance and, 45
Doctrines of risk, employer protection
    and, 161
Downsizing, 32, 34, 180
DPSP. *See* Deferred Profit Sharing Plans

Earnings, 5, 58
  instability of, 22, 25–26, 35–36
  job security as, insurance, 3–4
  managerial and professional, 34,
    35–36
  Medicaid coverage and, 85–86

preretirement, and social security,
    116–117, 121–123, 122t,
    125–126, 125t
  workers' compensation benefits
    based on, 162, 164
Education
  alternative employment and, 59, 60
  contingency employment and,
    57–58, 62
  earnings instability and, 25–26, 36
  health care coverage and, 87–88
  job stability and, 22, 29, 43
Employee Retirement Security Act
    (ERISA), 66
Employee–employer relationships, 123
  defined contribution plans and,
    116–117
  health care coverage, 16, 94–100,
    112
  risk shifting issues in, 1, 2–10, 83,
    97, 99, 132, 163
  workers' compensation, 162–163,
    167–170
Employees. *See* Workforce
Employers, 131
  bargaining power of, 43, 157n12
  demand-side vs. supply-side risks
    and, 2–3, 5–7, 42–45, 170–171
  insurance types provided by, 5–6, 45,
    162
  job creation vs. destruction by,
    37–38, 41
  pension coverage and, 83–84, 96f,
    132, 133–138, 145–147, 149–153
  plant closings by, 30, 32, 33–34
  protection of, 7–9, 64, 161, 162,
    176–180
  workers' compensation principles
    and, 175, 176–177
  See also Employee–employer
    relationships
Employment arrangements, 53–78
  Canada, 53, 68–72, 76, 77

Registered Pension Plans (RPP), 72,
133, 134, 153–154
Registered Retirement Savings Plans
(RRSP), 79n12, 121, 133–135,
144, 146–147, 151
Rehabilitation benefits, 162, 163,
178–179, 182
Repetitive strain injuries, 177, 181
Residential areas, health coverage and,
88
Retail sector, health coverage in, 92
Retirement age, early, 117, 123,
124–125
Retirement income, 45
annuities and, 118, 164–165
comparisons by country, 123–124,
132
income replacement by social
security systems, 124, 125t
Individual Retirement Account, 66,
79n12, 138, 146
life expectancy and, 117–118
pensions and, 65t, 66, 72, 79n12,
131–132, 141t, 147–149
risks in, 115–118, 124–126
Registered Retirement Savings Plan,
79n12, 121, 133–134, 135, 144,
146–147
social security systems and, 115–
129, 122t, 125t
taxes and, 122, 128, 143–144
workers' compensation benefits and,
164–165
See also Pension plans
Retirement Protection Act, PBGC
funding and, 155
Risk
employment arrangements and,
53–78
health care and, 83–113
labor markets and, 1–16, 117
measures of, 5, 115–116
pensions and, 116–118, 131–155
retirement income and, 115–118,
124–126

social security systems and, sharing,
115–129, 187
wage and job, for workers, 19–46,
117
workers' compensation and, shifting,
161–187
Royal Canadian Mounted Police,
pensions for, 135
RPP. *See* Registered Pension Plan
RRSP. *See* Registered Retirement
Savings Plans

Savings accounts
Individual Retirement Account, 66,
79n12, 138, 146
retirement income and, 119–120, 121
Registered Retirement Savings Plan,
79n12, 121, 133–135, 144, 146–
147, 151
Self-employed workers, 59, 61, 64, 79n4
in alternative workforce, 53, 56t
Canada, 68t, 69–71, 77–78, 79n10
in contingent workforce, 54–55, 57t
health care coverage for, 79n11, 91
U.S.A., 53–64, 69–70, 77
workers' compensation for, 164,
173–174, 176–177
Self-funded insurance
health coverage, 95, 97, 98, 102, 103
workers' compensation, 167
Service workers, 29, 43, 44, 92
business sector and, 54, 57t, 58, 62,
179
contingent employment and, 54, 57t,
58, 62, 179–180
high-risk industries and, 173–174
Single persons, 96f, 125t
retirement income of, 66, 121, 122t,
146
SIPP. *See* Survey of Income and
Program Participation
Social Security Disability Insurance (DI
or SSDI), 85, 175
Social Security in Canada, 118–129,
122t, 125t

Utilities sector, health coverage in, 93

Vesting requirements, pension plans and, 136
Vocational rehabilitation, 162, 163, 178–179, 182

Wages, 58
  benefits and, 92, 99, 127, 134, 141, 156n9–157n9
  collective bargaining and, 157n12
  declines in, 9, 29, 35–36, 163
  flexibility of, 10–11, 24–26, 38–39
  macroeconomic theories and, 41–42
  minimum, 4, 26
  risk and, 6, 8, 117, 161, 168–175
Washington (state), workers' compensation, 162, 179
Welfare state benefits
  Canada, 118–122, 122t, 124–129, 125t
  Europe, 1, 13, 123, 167
  government insurance, 4, 22–23, 40, 64, 84–87, 115–129, 122t
  paternalism in politics and, 43
  U.S.A., 1, 85–87, 119, 123–129, 125t
White workers, 25, 28–29, 31t, 58, 59, 90
Wisconsin, workers' compensation, 162
Worker Adjustment and Retraining Notification Act, 39
Workers' compensation, 14–15, 161–187
  Canada, 162, 163–167, 166f, 177–182, 184–186
  courts and, 161–162, 183–185
  danger pay, 169, 172–174
  exemptions from, 64, 164, 176–177, 180
  injury payments, 167–175
  law and legislation, 16, 161–164, 168, 169, 175–179, 182–185
  as mandated benefit, 63, 162, 168
  payments for, 175–176

principles underlying, 175–176
  reform backlash, 182–187, 187n6
  taxes and, 169–171, 172, 174
  U.S.A., 162–167, 166f, 175–184
Workforce, 161
  collectives within, 167 (*see also* Trade unions)
  demographics of, 7, 9, 45
  education of, 22, 25–26, 29, 43, 57–60, 62
  employment arrangements of, 57–60, 176–177
  employment regulations and, 4, 39
  health care coverage and, 83, 88–89, 100–101
  labor market risks for, 1, 2–10, 16, 19–46
  pension coverage of, 133–134, 138, 139–141, 141t, 156n9–157n9
  skill-biased technological change and, 22, 43
  training for, 39, 54, 73
  See also Age of workforce
Workplace hazards. *See* Occupational illnesses; Occupational injuries
WSPA, in OAS pension projections, 110

Yukon, workers' compensation, 164

About the Institute

The W.E. Upjohn Institute for Employment Research is a nonprofit research organization devoted to finding and promoting solutions to employment-related problems at the national, state, and local levels. It is an activity of the W.E. Upjohn Unemployment Trustee Corporation, which was established in 1932 to administer a fund set aside by the late Dr. W.E. Upjohn, founder of The Upjohn Company, to seek ways to counteract the loss of employment income during economic downturns.

The Institute is funded largely by income from the W.E. Upjohn Unemployment Trust, supplemented by outside grants, contracts, and sales of publications. Activities of the Institute comprise the following elements: 1) a research program conducted by a resident staff of professional social scientists; 2) a competitive grant program, which expands and complements the internal research program by providing financial support to researchers outside the Institute; 3) a publications program, which provides the major vehicle for disseminating the research of staff and grantees, as well as other selected works in the field; and 4) an Employment Management Services division, which manages most of the publicly funded employment and training programs in the local area.

The broad objectives of the Institute's research, grant, and publication programs are to 1) promote scholarship and experimentation on issues of public and private employment and unemployment policy, and 2) make knowledge and scholarship relevant and useful to policymakers in their pursuit of solutions to employment and unemployment problems.

Current areas of concentration for these programs include causes, consequences, and measures to alleviate unemployment; social insurance and income maintenance programs; compensation; workforce quality; work arrangements; family labor issues; labor-management relations; and regional economic development and local labor markets.